LEVEL 4

A Floral Arrangement

Ann Gianola

Richmond READERS

LEVEL 1

(500 headwords)

Maria's Dilemma
Oscar
Jack's Game
The Boy from Yesterday
The Black Mountain

LEVEL 2

(800 headwords)

Jason Causes Chaos
Craigen Castle Mystery
The Road through the Hills and othes stories
Where's Mauriac?
Saturday Storm

LEVEL 3

(1200 headwords)

A Trip to the Stars
Dr Jekyll and Mr Hyde
The Canterville Ghost and Other Stories
Cold Feet
Frankenstein
P.R. and Prejudice

LEVEL 4

(1800 headwords)

A Trip to London
Dracula   Jane Eyre
The Adventures of Tom Sawyer
Sense and Sensibility
William and Kate: A Royal Romance
Medical Match

LEVEL 5

(2600+ headwords)

Steve Jobs: the man behind Apple
Elizabeth II: The Diamond Queen
Sherlock Holmes & the Oxford murders

❧ Contents ☙

❧ Chapter 1 ❧

Julio's Flower Shop

Luisa carefully placed the last pale pink rose into the bouquet*. As she expertly positioned it between a white lily and a dark pink carnation, she admired her work. Then she cut a piece of silk ribbon, wound it around the center of the vase, and tied it into a bow. "Beautiful," she thought, as she turned the arrangement around on her worktable, inspecting it from every angle. "Perfect for the mother of a new baby girl." After deciding that the job was complete, Luisa picked the vase up and walked toward the refrigerated case. She put it inside with the other pretty flowers that celebrated a birthday, a wedding anniversary, and a job promotion. Everything was ready for the next round of deliveries, and Luisa knew that the recipients would be delighted.

For a moment, Luisa leaned her head forward and rubbed the tense muscles at the back of her neck. As the manager of *Julio's Flower Shop*, she often felt a lot of pressure. Today, however, things were going fairly well. Her three full-time employees were busy. Emma was helping the customers at the front counter. Katya was in the back, gathering the flowers and greenery for their next big order: two large displays for the lobby of the Piedmont Hotel. And Armando, the van driver, had just returned from the afternoon deliveries. "Perhaps I can even go home by 7:00p.m.," thought Luisa happily.

Luisa appreciated getting home at a reasonable hour. It felt great to walk upstairs to her apartment, located directly above the shop. She was relieved to be off her feet, even though the business remained on her mind. At night, she often sat and reviewed accounts on her computer. It was reassuring to see that *Julio's Flower Shop*—a relatively small, family-owned business—was surviving in these difficult economic times. However, Luisa's goal was not just to survive, but also to keep growing. She wanted to honor the memory of her beloved grandfather, *Abuelo* Julio, an immigrant from Mexico. He started this business nearly sixty years ago, selling flowers from a tiny stand on a street corner here in Santa Alicia.

Thirty years ago, Luisa's parents took over the business. By then, *Julio's Flower Shop* had moved into a small rented store. Then, about ten years ago, her family had bought a two-story building on 29th Street. In that location, Luisa began to help out during the summer when she was a teenager. She did a variety of tasks: loading and unloading the van, pruning and watering the flowers, answering phone calls and e-mails, waiting on customers, and sweeping the floor—a job that *never* ended. Of course, she made a few mistakes back then. Everyone laughed when she accidentally mixed up the personal-message cards for two bouquets. The card for the ninety-six-year-old woman read: "Love and kisses to my beautiful girlfriend." And the card for the twenty-three-year-old woman read: "Happy Birthday, Granny! You don't look a day over eighty."

In addition to being more careful about cards, Luisa learned a lot about the flower business from her parents. At work, she closely observed them. She watched how they created elegant floral arrangements by combining flowers according to color, shape, and size. She listened as they gave advice to customers about the kinds of flowers to buy for various life events, both happy and sad. Although Luisa left home to study business at the university, she had always wanted to return to *Julio's Flower Shop*. This was where she planned to use her knowledge. It was a family legacy*, and she was completely devoted to it.

Luisa's thoughts were interrupted by a telephone call. "There is someone on Line 1," Emma announced. "She wants to discuss flowers for her daughter's wedding."

"I'll take that," answered Luisa. "Thank you." She picked up the phone in the back of the shop. "This is Luisa Sánchez," she said politely. "How can I help you?"

"This is Amanda Brooks," boomed a voice on the other end of the line. "I've heard that you people do flowers."

"Yes, we do," replied Luisa cheerfully. "We've been in business for nearly sixty…"

"Never mind that," Mrs. Brooks interrupted. "I want to discuss some ideas for my daughter's wedding. It's in June."

"Certainly," said Luisa. "You're welcome to visit our shop on 29th Street or…"

"Never," said Mrs. Brooks. "I don't really care for that part of town. You need to come to *me*. I'm in Oak Hills." Luisa quickly wrote down Mrs. Brooks' address.

"Of course, I can also come to you," she said, looking through her appointment book. "Is next Monday okay? I can work around your schedule."

"Next Monday?" answered Mrs. Brooks. "Absolutely not. If you really want my business, you'll need to be here *tonight* at 7:00p.m."

"Oh, uh, yes! I can do that, too," Luisa answered, trying to sound happier than she really felt. She confirmed the time with Mrs. Brooks and hung up the phone. Luisa sighed. Clearly, she was no longer going home by 7:00p.m. She was going to Oak Hills.

❧ Chapter 2 ❧
A Trip to Oak Hills

Providing flowers for events was good for business at *Julio's Flower Shop*. A big wedding, for example, could bring in a lot of money. Over the years, the Sánchez family had provided flowers for many, many weddings. They were a labor of love—but also very profitable. Luisa would definitely go and meet Amanda Brooks at *her* place and time. After all, she lived in Oak Hills. Very wealthy people lived up there. They could spend thousands of dollars on an occasion like this. For that reason, Luisa didn't really consider this woman's horrible telephone manner. Besides, she had dealt with many rude people over the years. If Mrs. Brooks wanted a fairytale wedding for her daughter—with a lot of flowers— then Luisa would unquestionably meet her tonight.

At 5:00p.m., Luisa ran upstairs to shower and change her clothes. She put on her black skirt, matching jacket, and a freshly ironed white blouse. Then she looked at herself in the mirror. "I think the hair needs to go up," she thought, sweeping her long brown hair into a bun and pinning it behind her head. "That's better. A more formal look for Oak Hills." Finally, Luisa gathered a few things to put into her briefcase. The first was her laptop. Luisa had spent months designing the website for *Julio's Flower Shop*. On the computer, she could easily show Mrs. Brooks dozens of flower varieties, photos from other weddings, testimonials* from clients, a history of the business, and more. She also packed a black portfolio* that contained more impressive photos and documents, and last, but not least, she inserted a contract. After all, it was already April.

June was just two months away. Mrs. Brooks was probably anxious to find a florist.

Shortly after 6:00p.m., Luisa walked through the shop. She thanked Katya for locking up for her. "No problem," Katya said. "I'll return the keys through your mail slot." Then Luisa walked by Emma as she was checking receipts at the front counter.

"You look great!" said Emma. "And good luck with that client. Sell her everything. Remember, rich people need to show off in front of their friends."

"Thanks," said Luisa. "I'll do my best."

"I just put gas in the small van," said Armando, opening the front door for her. "You can get to Oak Hills and back a dozen times."

"I really hope it's only *once*," said Luisa, waving. "Thank you!"

Luisa carefully drove north. About forty-five minutes later, she was driving along the beautiful tree-lined streets of Oak Hills. "Amazing homes," she thought, as she passed one enormous house after another. "These places are slightly bigger than my apartment above the shop," she laughed to herself.

Luisa checked her directions and turned off on a small private road that eventually led to a very large iron gate. She stopped the van, pressed a button on an intercom*, and heard a man's voice.

"Who is it, please?"

"This is Luisa Sánchez from *Julio's Flower Shop*. I have an appointment with Mrs. Brooks." The gate swung open slowly, allowing for her van to pass through to the other side. Luisa continued until she reached a long driveway beside a white limestone mansion*. Surrounded by gigantic oak trees, this incredible home had Greek columns, wraparound balconies, and arched windows. A while ago, Luisa had seen pictures of this estate in a magazine. Now, even after the sun had set, it was astonishing to see it in person. "Wow!" she thought. "This is *the* Brooks Mansion."

Before Luisa stepped out of the car, she took one last look at herself in the rearview mirror. "No spinach in my teeth," she reassured herself. She felt a little nervous and took a deep breath. She had never met a customer in a place like this. "Pretend that this is just another house and another prospective client," Luisa said to her reflection. "Do your best to convince Amanda Brooks to go with *Julio's Flower Shop*. And come back with a signed contract."

❧ Chapter 3 ☙

A Chance Meeting

Luisa stepped out of the van. It was getting quite dark now, but she could see a lovely rose garden on each side of the long walkway that led to the house. The roses weren't blooming yet, but Luisa knew that they would be spectacular* in two months. "Just in time for the wedding," she thought.

"Glad to meet you, Ryan," said Luisa, extending her hand.

"May I help you?" called a voice from the rose garden. A man dressed in a T-shirt and jeans approached her. He had a rake in his hands.

"Oh, hello," said Luisa. "I'm Luisa Sánchez...the florist... here to see Amanda Brooks."

"Of course you are," he said, flashing a warm smile and putting down the rake. "She's expecting you. Come with me. I'm Ryan Soto, by the way."

"Glad to meet you, Ryan," said Luisa, extending her hand.

"Excuse me," said Ryan. "I'd really like to shake your hand, but I'm a mess. You don't want dirt on your nice clothes."

"Okay," said Luisa, dropping her hand, "if you say so. But I must say that your garden is magnificent. I can't imagine the work that goes into caring for a place like this."

"A *lot* of work, yes," said Ryan, turning toward Luisa. "Fortunately, I'm not the only gardener here. I'm in charge of the roses, though. On this estate, there are hundreds of bushes to take care of."

"Well," said Luisa. "I'd love to see them in the daylight— especially in June when they're all blooming."

"Hopefully you can," said Ryan, taking Luisa up the steps to the front door. Now Luisa could see him clearly in the lights that shone from the outdoor lamps. He was a very tall and handsome man, no more than thirty years old. He had dark hair, greenish-brown eyes, and an athletic build. His expression was very kind. "Sorry, I'm not allowed in the house," he said, twisting the large doorknob, "but you go in."

"Are you sure about that?" asked Luisa, wondering if she should really enter the home through the open door.

"Yes, I'm sure. Go ahead," said Ryan, directing her toward the foyer*. "She'll be down any moment. Good luck!" Then Ryan leaned closer to Luisa and whispered, "Don't let her frighten you." He smiled at her again and then left, closing the front door behind him. Luisa was standing alone now. She took a moment to admire the beautiful white marble floors, the crystal chandelier and the sweeping staircase, before a woman appeared at the top of the stairs.

"And *who* are you?" she asked loudly.

"Oh, good evening," said Luisa, looking up. "I'm Luisa Sánchez from…"

"Yes, right. The florist," the woman said, walking slowly down the stairs. "I'm Amanda Brooks. And *how* did you get inside my home?" she asked, with annoyance.

"Ryan, uh, your gardener, let me in. I'm so sorry if…"

"Ugh! My *gardener* let you in," she said, impatiently. "He didn't come inside, did he?"

"No, he didn't," Luisa answered, looking down at the floor and feeling embarrassed.

"Good. I can't have…that…in my house."

Luisa was shocked. Mrs. Brooks was worse than she had imagined. Was she actually living in the twenty-first century? How could she speak about an employee with such contempt*? Mrs. Brooks clearly drew lines between her social class and Ryan's. Luisa felt disgusted, but didn't say anything. "Follow me," said Mrs. Brooks, leading Luisa into a sitting room on the first floor.

If it weren't for her ugly behavior, Mrs. Brooks might have been a very pretty older woman. She was in her mid-fifties, her dark brown hair shoulder-length with just a few streaks of gray. She had soft green eyes that were much kinder than the way she spoke.

Mrs. Brooks sat down in a comfortable armchair. Then she pointed to a smaller, harder chair for Luisa. "First, you must know that I've already been through three florists. The first two were completely incompetent*, so I fired them. And the third one—located right here in Oak Hills—refused to work with me after our first meeting. Can you believe that?" Luisa didn't answer. But she could, in fact, believe it. Mrs. Brooks suddenly stood up and began to walk around the room. "My daughter's wedding is in less than two months. I have to do *something*! Darcy Blackwell, a friend from my rose garden club, used your business for her holiday party last year. I must say, the flowers looked, well, rather acceptable."

"Thank you," replied Luisa. Silently, however, she thought, "*Your* rose garden club? You wouldn't have a rose garden without Ryan's hard work. And yet, he isn't allowed inside your home."

❧ Chapter 4 ❧

The Formidable Mrs. Brooks

Luisa's parents always stressed the value of an education. Luisa and her two older brothers, Arturo and Felipe, were continually reminded about the importance of school. Pedro and Beatriz Sánchez never allowed their children to work in the shop if it interfered with their studies. They wanted them to attend universities. They wanted them to have opportunities in life. "Study hard," said Luisa's father to all of his children. "Become professionals. Live the *American Dream*."

"Yes, Papá," Luisa replied. "I promise to study hard. But you and Mamá are successful. You own this building. You are living the *American Dream*."

Luisa's mother shook her head. "We are proud, *mija*," said Beatriz. "But we must work our fingers to the bone." She frowned at the sight of her own worn hands. "We want your lives to be easier." Then she went in to talk about the other members of their family. "Look at your *tíos* and *tías*, Luisa. Their lives have been even more difficult. They have always worked for rich people raising *their* children, cleaning *their* houses, cooking *their* food, and doing *their* gardening. And they make very little money. They don't have—and never will have—your chance at something better."

Luisa and her brothers obeyed their parents. They were exceptional students. They were all admitted to good universities. And all three received scholarships from a local foundation* that supported high-achieving Latinos. Now, at twenty-nine, Arturo was a successful attorney. At twenty-seven, Felipe was a mechanical engineer. And at twenty-five, Luisa, at her insistence, was the full-time manager of *Julio's Flower Shop*. Her administrative skills and familiarity with the business allowed her parents to semi-retire. They were freed from the grueling* seventy-hour workweeks. Their dreams for their children—and for themselves—had come true.

Luisa saw that the road to success was a long one. It took three generations* for her family to become established in this country. However, they proved that it could be done, and Luisa was determined to share this message. In fact, last month the *Times Journal* had done a feature article about the Sánchez family. It told the story of *Julio's Flower Shop*, from its humble beginnings on a street corner to the successful business that it was today. The article contained many photographs, including a lovely one of Luisa standing in the doorway of the shop on 29th Street. Of course, the publicity was wonderful for business. But Luisa also hoped the story would be an inspiration for other immigrants.

Luisa kept a copy of that article inside a plastic cover in her portfolio. At the end of a very long, tedious* conversation with Mrs. Brooks on the subject of her daughter's wedding, Luisa pulled it out and gave it to her. She wanted to show Mrs. Brooks that *Julio's Flower Shop* was a good company, owned and operated by honest, reliable, and hardworking people. "Hmm," said Mrs. Brooks, without great interest. "Yes, I'll take a look at that later. But let's get back to the wedding, shall we? I'm afraid you must return here early next week and meet my daughter, Sarah. She'll have some opinions, too."

"Okay," said Luisa. "I'll be happy to do that. So, Mrs. Brooks, am I your new florist?" she asked, reaching inside her briefcase for a contract.

"Yes," Mrs. Brooks sighed, opening a desk drawer and removing her checkbook. "I suppose so. It's getting late. I don't have much choice anymore, do I? How much do you need—and where do I sign?"

It was after 9:00p.m. when Luisa finally walked out of the front door. She couldn't believe that Ryan was still out in the garden, raking by the light of a portable* lamp. Ryan looked up as Luisa made her way down the path. He put down his rake and walked toward her. "How did it go?" he asked, curiously.

"Okay, I think," replied Luisa. "I need to come back in a few days and meet her daughter."

"That's a good sign," said Ryan, encouragingly. "And you'll like Sarah. She's very nice and easygoing—the complete opposite of her mother. And don't worry. Mrs. Brooks will calm down eventually. She's just like the expression: *Her bark is worse than her bite.*"

"If you say so," said Luisa, rolling her eyes. "But I see you're still slaving away in this rose garden. People do need sleep, you know."

"Well," said Ryan, taking a longer look at Luisa's pretty face in the moonlight, "everything needs to be perfect for Sarah's wedding reception because… come to think of it… that woman's bite can still be very painful."

❧ Chapter 5 ❧

Feelings Revealed

Julio's Flower Shop was closed on a Sunday. On that day, Luisa's parents frequently had afternoon gatherings at their home. Although many of their relatives lived in Mexico, usually twenty or so family members and friends got together and enjoyed plenty of delicious Mexican food: *carne asada tacos, tamales, arroz, frijoles,* and *guacamole.* Luisa watched as her mother and *Tia* Teresa, both wonderful cooks, prepared their amazing *salsa* in the kitchen.

"*Hermana,*" said Beatriz to her sister, "I think it needs a little more *cilantro* and *jalapeño* pepper. Don't you agree, *mija*? Taste it."

"Sorry," said Luisa. "What did you say?"

"You're daydreaming again, Luisa," laughed her aunt, adding a few more ingredients to the *salsa.* "What's on your mind? Did you have a hard week at work?"

"Well, I had a very strange week, that's for sure," Luisa said, as her aunt poured the delicious red mixture into a bowl.

"And there is a little smile on your face, Luisa. *Qué pasó?* Tell us everything."

"We have a new client," said Luisa, dipping a tortilla chip into the *salsa* and taking a bite. "Her name is Amanda Brooks. She lives in Oak Hills. She's ordering a lot of flowers for her daughter's wedding in June. It may be the biggest account we've ever had."

"Great news!" said her aunt, passing her a napkin. "How is the *salsa*?"

"It's incredible," replied Luisa, wiping her mouth. "Perfect. Don't add another thing."

"Yes, now it's good," agreed Beatriz, tasting it again. "Now, tell your *tia* what she said about the gardener."

"Well, when I told her that the, um, *very* nice gardener had let me inside, Mrs. Brooks was angry that he might have entered the house. '*He didn't come inside, did he? I can't have… that…in my house!*'" Luisa mimicked. "Can you believe it?"

"*Ay*, Luisa," said her aunt. "I can believe it. I've seen and heard it all. Do you remember that woman I worked for several years ago? I was her housekeeper and nanny. She barely let her own children inside the house. '*Teresa*,' she said. '*Take the kids to the park! They're so loud! My nerves!*' Then she would cuddle her crazy little dog and kiss *him* on the lips!" At this, both Luisa and Beatriz roared with laughter. "But I want to hear more about the *very* nice gardener," continued Teresa. At the mention of Ryan, Luisa blushed.

"Do you have something to tell us, Luisa?" asked her mother. "You're not *mixing business with pleasure*, are you?"

"No!" said Luisa, her face turning redder still. "He was just a really pleasant guy. We talked about the rose garden that he labors in, day and night, in fear of Mrs. Brooks."

"And he was handsome, too, I suppose," laughed Teresa. "Does he have big muscles from all of that hard work?" Teresa continued to laugh, but Luisa's mother became rather serious.

"Be careful, my dear," said Beatriz, quietly. "I'm sure your client's gardener is a very nice young man, but please focus on our business—not theirs. Besides, a rose garden is not where you should be looking for a serious relationship."

"Your mother is right," added Teresa. "You're much better off finding a lawyer or a mechanical engineer. I'm sure your brothers know some decent single men at work with more solid careers. Smaller muscles, perhaps, but you'll be more comfortable in the long run."

Luisa put her hands on her waist and felt a sudden surge of anger.

"Thank you both for your concern," she said curtly*. "First of all, I don't have time for a serious relationship. Secondly, if I did have time, I would not need help from either of my brothers. And finally, have you forgotten that many of our relatives are manual laborers—or began that way? Is that really so dishonorable*?" Luisa was visibly upset. She poured herself a glass of water and took a drink. "From this family," she added, "I have learned that it's important to judge a person by his character—and not by his occupation." Then Luisa abruptly turned away from her mother and aunt and walked out of the kitchen. Beatriz and Teresa stared at each other in disbelief. When they could see that Luisa was safely out of earshot, Teresa turned to her sister.

"Well," she said. "I think we just learned a very valuable lesson, didn't we?"

"We certainly did," replied Beatriz. "*Dios, mío.* My daughter is in love with a gardener!"

❧ Chapter 6 ☙

A Second Meeting

The following week, Luisa had to return to Oak Hills. She was able to get dressed and leave the shop by 4:00p.m., but she still felt tired after another very busy day. She dreaded having to deal with Mrs. Brooks again. But, according to Ryan, her daughter was *the complete opposite of her mother.* "Good thing," she thought, enjoying the memory of their recent conversation. "I wish they were both a little more like Ryan." Luisa felt her face getting warmer. It wasn't the first time that she had thought about Mrs. Brooks' very good-natured *and* good-looking gardener. She would prefer talking to him than to either of them. Nevertheless, as she drove through the iron gate, she tried to concentrate on the high-paying contract for the wedding.

Luisa parked the van in the long driveway next to the house. She got out of the van and immediately looked in the direction of the rose garden. When she didn't see Ryan working among the bushes, she felt a pang of disappointment. However, her spirits lifted instantly when she turned toward the house and saw him drinking a bottle of water on the front steps. As Luisa headed toward Ryan, smiles quickly appeared on both of their faces. "Taking a break?" Luisa asked, playfully. "I hope it's not a long one. Those roses can't prune themselves."

"Hello again," said Ryan, standing up. This time, he stretched out his strong right hand and shook hers gently. "Don't worry," he said. "I just washed my hands, so you won't get dirty."

"I wasn't worried," said Luisa, gazing down indifferently* at her stylish green dress and black sweater. Luisa let go of his hand, and Ryan sat down on the steps again. Right away he turned his attention back to her, taking note of her lovely face and the long brown hair that was pulled back into a decorative barrette*.

"I must tell you," he said, putting the cap back on his water bottle, "I read that article about your family in the *Times Journal* last month. It was very inspiring."

"Oh, did you see that?" asked Luisa, slightly embarrassed, but also quite pleased.

"I did," said Ryan. "I really liked it. There was a nice picture of you, too," he added, "although the real-life version is even better." Luisa nervously shifted her briefcase from one hand to the other, but enjoyed the compliment. "Also, you should know that the article gave hope to struggling entrepreneurs*—like me," he said, pointing to the words printed on his T-shirt: *Soto Landscape Architecture.*

"Really?" said Luisa, taking a step closer to get a better look. "Is that your business?"

"Yes," said Ryan, shyly, "it's all mine. But it's pretty small at this point. I started it about a year and a half ago. I've had some clients, but business isn't exactly booming. So far, I'm the only employee."

"Still, that's wonderful," said Luisa. "Congratulations."

"Someday," added Ryan, standing up and brushing some dirt off his jeans, "I hope it grows bigger. It may never be in the same league as *Julio's Flower Shop*," he said, gesturing toward Luisa's van, "but you never know." Once again, Ryan looked into Luisa's beautiful brown eyes and saw her genuine interest in what he had to say.

"We're still a rather small company, Ryan," said Luisa. "And our success didn't happen overnight. My grandfather started the business a very long time ago."

"I realize that," admitted Ryan. "I must continually remind myself that *Rome wasn't built in a day*, but sometimes it's frustrating. I have the experience—and a lot of ideas. It's just a really tough time to launch a business."

"Speaking of business," Luisa sighed, looking at her watch. "I should probably go into the house and talk to Mrs. Brooks and her daughter now."

"And I should get back to my roses," he said, picking up his gardening gloves and pruning shears*. "Very nice to talk to you, Luisa. Perhaps we can talk again—about business or something." He stomped some dirt from the bottom of his boots. "Uh, may I…uh, could I…perhaps call you sometime?"

"Sure," said Luisa, her knees suddenly feeling a little wobbly. She hoped that she wouldn't fall over in her black high-heeled shoes. "I'd really like that."

"Ugh!" said Ryan, patting the pockets of his jeans. "I don't have my phone with me—or a pencil and paper."

"You can almost always find me at *Julio's Flower Shop*," said Luisa. "Our phone number is on the website. Or you can look at the side of my van. The number is right there."

"Great!" said Ryan, standing straight up and quickly descending the steps. "I'll take a look at the number right now—and memorize it."

❧ Chapter 7 ❧
Flower Talk

As Luisa walked up the steps to the front door, she couldn't stop a huge grin from spreading across her face. "He wants to call me!" she thought to herself excitedly. She resisted the urge to turn around and look at his handsome figure walking away. As she rang the front doorbell, Luisa began to reflect on Ryan's expanding list of good qualities. She now knew that he was more than just a pleasant—and incredibly attractive—guy who worked in a rose garden. He was also kind, considerate, and enterprising*. Perhaps even a future business mogul*. "And in the light of day, even more attractive," Luisa thought, trying to contain the giggle that desperately wanted to escape from her mouth. Suddenly, the front door swung open and revealed someone wearing a very cross expression. It was Mrs. Brooks.

"What's so funny?" Mrs. Brooks demanded, looking at Luisa suspiciously. Luisa immediately covered her mouth, while Mrs. Brooks' eyes darted back and forth between Luisa at her front door and Ryan in the distance. Now, Luisa had to turn around. She could see that Ryan was strolling back toward the rose garden from the parked van. He was muttering a list of numbers that Luisa suspected was the telephone number of her shop. Mrs. Brooks narrowed her eyes and glared at Luisa.

"Nothing's funny, really," Luisa stammered, trying to distract Mrs. Brooks. "Uh, I was just thinking about..." Mrs. Brooks waved her hand dismissively.

"Never mind," she said. "Come in. Sarah has been waiting for you." Mrs. Brooks led Luisa into the same room on the first floor where they had sat before. Inside was a young woman of about twenty-four. Sarah had an open, honest expression. She was tall and blonde and wasn't wearing any makeup. She quickly stood up, shook Luisa's hand, and introduced herself. "Hello, Miss Sánchez. I'm Sarah Brooks. Lovely to meet you," she said.

"It's very nice to meet you, Miss. Brooks," said Luisa, sensing immediately that Sarah was indeed the complete opposite of her mother.

"Oh, please call me *Sarah*," she said. "And thank you so much for coming all this way to meet with us. I think you had to travel a fair distance, didn't you?" Then Sarah went on to apologize for not looking her best. She was barefoot and dressed very informally in a white cotton blouse and denim skirt. "I've been out in the garden today."

"Not to worry," said Luisa. "You look great. And please call me *Luisa*."

"Enough chitchat!" cried Mrs. Brooks irritably. "We have a lot to accomplish* tonight." Luisa immediately stopped talking, opened her briefcase, and picked up her notes from their last meeting.

"We had been talking about the centerpiece at the head table," recalled Mrs. Brooks, grabbing a round peppermint candy from a bowl on the table and unwrapping it. "I want the roses, orchids, lilies, and everything else to be cascading down the front of the table," she added, her arms circling dramatically. "I'm also picturing bowls of flowers—lots of them—surrounded by floating candles. And I want the whole area, table and floor, to be scattered with rose petals. Are you writing this down?"

"Oh, yes," said Luisa, scribbling notes as fast as she could. "I'm following you." Mrs. Brooks popped the hard candy into her mouth and sucked noisily on it. Then she began to walk around the room.

"You remember that this reception will be in a huge tent on our property, overlooking the rose garden," said Mrs. Brooks, moving the candy around in her mouth. "Inside, there will thirty tables—ten people at each one—for the three hundred guests that we expect. Now, for those tables…"

Meanwhile, Sarah pressed her hands together and cleared her throat. "You know, Mom," she said, very sincerely. "I don't want this to be too over-the-top. Do we really need the flowers to be *cascading*? Are floating candles and rose petals everywhere absolutely necessary? I think the décor might be a bit much, considering the tent is right next to a gorgeous rose garden. How will people eat with all of that stuff on the table? Seriously, I'd be fine with something very *simple*." Mrs. Brooks stopped walking, looked down at her daughter, and gasped in horror.

"Okay, Mom," said Sarah hurriedly, realizing that her mother was infuriated*. "We can have it your way, but let's tone it down just a bit, shall we? What do you think, Luisa?" Luisa, however, hadn't heard a word that Sarah said. She had already leapt out of her chair to assist Mrs. Brooks, who was no longer voicing her opinion about flowers—or anything else. She was choking.

🌿 Chapter 8 🌿

Luisa Saves a Life

"Are you all right?" asked Luisa, as Mrs. Brooks desperately clutched at her throat, a panicked look on her face. Sarah looked completely confused.

"Truly, Mom. I'm sorry," Sarah implored. "We can have rose petals six inches deep in the tent if you want, I was only trying to…" It was impossible for Mrs. Brooks to respond because she wasn't breathing at all.

"Sarah, please!" Luisa interrupted. "This isn't about the flowers! Your mother is choking!" she said, as she delivered blows to Mrs. Brooks' back, between her shoulder blades, with the heel of her hand. Both Luisa and Sarah fearfully saw that Mrs. Brooks' lips had already begun to turn blue. "I know the Heimlich Maneuver*," said Luisa, with authority. "But you need to get help!" Sarah stood frozen as Luisa swiftly positioned herself directly behind Mrs. Brooks, wrapping her arms around her waist. Then she made a fist and placed the thumb side of it against Mrs. Brooks' upper abdomen. As she grasped her fist with the other hand, she performed five quick but forceful upward thrusts, almost lifting Mrs. Brooks off the ground in the process. "Hurry!" Luisa shouted, as Sarah still remained motionless, almost as if she, too, couldn't breathe.

At last, Sarah ran out of the room. "Please call 911!" she shrieked to someone on the first floor. "My mother is choking! Ryan! *Where* is Ryan?" Luisa was entirely focused on her attempts to help Mrs. Brooks. She didn't hear the sound of someone making an emergency phone call, or the front door opening, or Sarah screaming Ryan's name again

"I know the Heimlich Maneuver!"

and again. She just repeated the maneuver she had already performed on Mrs. Brooks. Finally, after many blows and thrusts, the peppermint candy that had obstructed Mrs. Brooks' airway became dislodged. It came flying out of her mouth like a rocket.

Mrs. Brooks crumpled into a chair and began gasping and sobbing uncontrollably. But she was actually breathing again, thank goodness. Luisa felt completely drained by this frightening experience. Once the rush of adrenaline had left her body, she sank into the smaller chair across from Mrs. Brooks, her heart still racing. Then she gently reached for Mrs. Brooks' trembling hand. "You'll be okay," said Luisa, holding it in her own. "The candy is out now. Just try to relax and breathe normally." With her other hand, Luisa reached into her briefcase, brought out a tissue and softly wiped Mrs. Brooks' dripping eyes and nose. While Mrs. Brooks was still very distressed, her breathing gradually began to sound more normal. Just then, Sarah and Ryan came sprinting into the room. "Cancel the emergency call," said Luisa, still holding Mrs. Brooks' hand. "We got it out," she continued, getting another tissue and picking up the candy from the floor. "I'll just put this in the trash."

"Throw them all in the trash!" Mrs. Brooks croaked.

"Oh, Mom!" cried Sarah, tearfully embracing her mother. "I'm so happy that you're alive!"

"Are you okay?" asked Ryan, the alarmed expression on his face fading into relief.

"No, but I will be...eventually," said Mrs. Brooks in a raspy voice, giving a little nod to Luisa. "I'm just so... embarrassed."

"Well, people don't actually die of embarrassment, like they sometimes do from choking," said Sarah. "Luisa,

I appreciate you saving my mother's life," she declared emotionally. Then she walked over and gave Luisa a very heartfelt hug. "We really don't know how to thank you. And to think, I just sat there with no idea of what to do. One moment we're discussing cascading floral arrangements and the next my mother is choking to death!"

"By the way," interrupted Mrs. Brooks in a whisper, "When it's time for my actual funeral, I want cascading flowers all over the place. Promise me that, Sarah. Nothing *simple*."

"I promise, Mom. But I think you should go upstairs and rest now, okay?" said Sarah. "We can talk about flowers for weddings and funerals another day."

"Yes, you'll need to come back tomorrow or the next day, I suppose," said Mrs. Brooks, looking at Luisa and attempting to straighten up in her chair. "I've been through quite enough."

"Or, I could drive you to *Julio's Flower Shop* for the next meeting," interjected Ryan helpfully. "Your shop is on 29th Street, right? I know that part of town very well. Perhaps that would be easier for Luisa." At once, the sweet, subdued Mrs. Brooks disappeared. She instantly returned to the bad-tempered, condescending* woman she was before she nearly died.

"What have I told you about setting foot in my house, young man?" she barked. "You can see that I'm perfectly well here. Now, *get out!*"

❧ Chapter 9 ☙
Luisa Quits

It was late when Luisa finally turned the key in the lock of her apartment door. She switched on the light and put her briefcase on the floor. She was physically and emotionally exhausted from the whole ordeal at Mrs. Brooks' home. She knew that she should hang up her work clothes, put on her comfortable, well-worn sweats, and heat up her mother's delicious leftover chicken *fajitas*. Instead, however, she plopped down on the sofa, stared at the wall, and attempted to process the events of the bizarre evening in Oak Hills.

Of course, Luisa was happy that she had saved a person's life. The fact that she had taken a first aid class in high school, including a demonstration of the Heimlich Maneuver, was very fortunate indeed. The choking incident was certainly one of the most terrifying moments of her life, and Luisa was grateful that it hadn't ended tragically. "Mrs. Brooks lives on," thought Luisa, "if only to belittle her poor gardener another day."

Luisa took off her shoes and threw them in the direction of the door. She angrily remembered Ryan's downcast expression when Mrs. Brooks ordered him out of her home. It was clearly humiliating for him. How could she speak so disdainfully* to another human being—and after almost dropping dead? Was his blue-collar job* just too far beneath her? Luisa had also noticed that Ryan had a Latino surname. She wondered if Mrs. Brooks disliked people of his race and culture. "In that case, she would also dislike me," thought Luisa. "Perhaps she does, but must tolerate me because she's desperate for a florist. Therefore, I am allowed in the house—as long as I don't sit down on the nicer furniture." It all made sense to Luisa now, and it made her feel sick to her stomach.

It wasn't the first time Luisa had experienced prejudice. As a Mexican-American born in the U.S., she had definitely heard some offensive comments about her ancestry*. Even though they taught *tolerance* in her high school, there were a couple of kids who taunted her. "How did you get to school today?" asked one of them. "Did you swim across the river or crawl under the border fence?" When the principal announced that Luisa was the salutatorian, the second best graduate in her class, another girl asked, "Why try so hard? You don't have to be *that* smart to scrub floors." Luisa remembered the feelings of rage that those words ignited*. When she came home angry and tearful, her father said, "There is nothing you can say to those idiots, Luisa. Just ignore them. Don't stoop to their level." So Luisa didn't retaliate* with nasty remarks about *their* ethnicities or failing grades. She swallowed her pride and said nothing.

Luisa recalled other stories of injustices suffered by people in her family. *Tio* Juan was an agricultural worker when he first came to the U.S. His employer repeatedly cheated him out of money, believing that Juan wasn't smart enough to know the difference. Because Juan had to eat and support his family, he never complained. *Tia* Carmen, a hotel housekeeper for many years, was almost arrested when a guest accused her of stealing an expensive watch from his room. The hotel manager and the police questioned her for two hours. They threatened to fire her and send her to jail if she didn't return the watch. Later, the guest found the missing watch on the floor behind the nightstand. After a half-hearted apology from the manager, *Tia* Carmen went back to work and never spoke of it again.

Luisa's blood began to boil. Even though it was now after 10:00p.m., she picked up her cell phone and called her parents' home. Her mother picked up after the first ring. "*Qué pasó?*" she said. "Did someone die?"

"No," Luisa fumed. "But I almost wish someone did."

"*Mija*, what are you talking about?" asked Beatriz.

"I'm just back from Oak Hills again, Mamá—for the last time."

"What happened? Did that woman fire you?"

"No. But I'm thinking of firing her," said Luisa, breathing loudly into the phone. "I can't stand the way Mrs. Brooks mistreats her gardener." Luisa could hear her mother clucking her tongue over the line. "It's a long story, but she ordered him out of her home tonight when he was just trying to be helpful in an emergency."

"Wait a minute, *mija*," said Beatriz. "You need to calm down. Please don't let a little crush* on this gardener come between you and thousands of dollars for *Julio's Flower Shop*."

"I can't believe you just said that, Mamá. I'm hanging up now."

"Luisa," begged Beatriz, "We're running a business. It isn't your place to get involved in their relationship."

"Yes, it is my business. I can no longer say *nothing* about these things. It's time to stand up to bullies like her, Mamá. I refuse to do business with Amanda Brooks."

❧ Chapter 10 ❧
Beatriz Takes Control

It was impossible for Luisa to sleep that night. She tossed and turned for hours, haunted by Mrs. Brooks' cruel words and the wounded look on Ryan's face. She was now very glad that Mrs. Brooks was alive, so that she could hear the news that Luisa planned to deliver in the morning: "I'm tearing up your contract. I don't do business with elitists* and racists." Luisa enjoyed the idea of standing up to Mrs. Brooks. That woman could find another person to do the flowers for her daughter's silly wedding. There were a few florists left in Santa Alicia. Mrs. Brooks could abuse one of them instead. "Hire someone else to scatter rose petals and cower in fear," she thought. Luisa was finished swallowing her pride.

When Luisa finally went downstairs at 7:00a.m., there were two messages on the answering machine in the shop. She pushed the button and heard a familiar voice. "Hi, Luisa. It's Ryan Soto. You were amazing last night! Thanks for saving my, uh, employer. She may not show it, but she is very appreciative. We all are. Talk to you soon!" Luisa couldn't believe her ears. How could Ryan forgive Mrs. Brooks for degrading* him like that? Then Luisa listened to the second message. "Hi! It's Ryan, again. Sarah has convinced her mother to visit your shop on 29th Street. I'll be happy to bring them as neither one really likes to drive. We can come whenever it's convenient for you. Mrs. Brooks wants *you* to pick the time. I guess that's the least she can do for the person who saved her life! Anyway, call me back. Thanks! Looking forward to seeing you again!"

Luisa walked away from the answering machine in disgust. Suddenly, the *incredibly attractive* Ryan became much less attractive to her. She didn't like hearing the pleasant tone in his voice. She didn't like that he was willing to drive Mrs. Brooks and her daughter here and there because they were too lazy to do it themselves. Ryan should have been furious. Last night, he should have dug up every last rose bush in her garden. Then he should have driven straight through that ridiculous iron gate without waiting for it to swing open. Well, perhaps the destruction of Mrs. Brooks' property was a bad idea. But at the very least he should have stormed out of that house and never, ever returned. For Luisa, Ryan's submissive* behavior was unbearable. While she admitted that Ryan had many fine qualities, he was missing an essential one: self-respect. This was something that Luisa couldn't overlook. She really didn't want to see *any* of these people ever again.

Just then, the telephone in the shop rang. Fearing that it could be a third call from Ryan, Luisa did not pick up. "Luisa," said her mother's voice from the answering machine, "it's Mamá. Are you in the shop? If you're there, please answer." Luisa reached for the phone.

"Yes," she said, picking up the receiver. "I'm here."

"I hope you haven't broken the contract with Mrs. Brooks in Oak Hills. I worried about it all night. Let me handle her. I'm tough. I've handled worse people, I'm sure."

"Whatever," said Luisa, sighing deeply. "You and Papá are still the owners of this business, so you can do what you want. However, I will no longer be involved with this account. I can't deal with these people, okay? I'm done. I do not want any contact with Mrs. Brooks, her daughter, or her gardener."

"Her gardener? *Mija*, her gardener is the least of our problems! Remember, Mrs. Brooks signed a contract with us. We are now *legally* obliged to carry out the service we promised to deliver. If we refuse to honor the contract, she will call her attorneys and take us to court. And even with your brother's help, we will lose! We cannot risk that, Luisa. For sixty years, our family has worked to build this business and uphold our reputation. A lawsuit from a woman like that could ruin us."

Luisa looked up from the phone. She could see Katya standing at the front door, waiting for Luisa to let her in. Suddenly, Luisa felt an enormous wave of guilt. Her mother was right, of course. Mrs. Brooks was definitely the type to be vindictive. If she wished, she had the power to destroy *Julio's Flower Shop*. Luisa's parents could lose everything they had worked for. Her employees could lose their jobs. Katya depended on her salary from *Julio's Flower Shop* to support her son. Luisa waved at Katya and walked toward the entrance of the shop. She remained on the phone with her mother as she unlocked the front door.

"Good morning!" Katya said, walking toward the back to begin work.

"Good morning to you," said Luisa. "Okay, Mamá," she said, returning to the call. "So you'll deal with Mrs. Brooks. But I've really got to go now. Katya is here, and we have a lot to do."

"Perfect," said Beatriz. "I'll be in the shop in two hours. I'll call her and arrange everything. Don't worry about this account, *mija*. I've dealt with dozens of high-maintenance* people. They don't scare me a bit. In a few days," she laughed, "I'll have Mrs. Brooks and her daughter eating out of the palm of my hand."

✤ Chapter 11 ✤

A History of Julio's

Pedro and Beatriz Sánchez still worked part time at *Julio's Flower Shop*. They each put in about twenty hours a week, but it felt like a vacation compared to the twelve-hour days that they used to work. Pedro continued to do business with their wholesale flower dealers early in the morning, and Beatriz helped out with various tasks in the shop. Although her floral arrangements were masterful, her real strength was in personal service. The regular customers adored her and were disappointed when she wasn't there. Since she enjoyed both socializing and making sales, Beatriz tried to spend three or four hours in the shop most weekdays.

As promised, Beatriz arrived in the shop by 9:00 a.m. She went directly to Luisa and asked for all of the information on the big account in Oak Hills. Luisa opened a file drawer and happily handed over everything: Mrs. Brooks' contract, her personal information, and all of the notes on Sarah's wedding so far. "It's all yours, Mamá!" said Luisa, as if she couldn't let go of it fast enough. "Good luck with that!" Beatriz eagerly took the file. Then she went straight upstairs to the studio apartment next to Luisa's above the shop.

Ten years ago, when Pedro and Beatriz bought the building on 29th Street, they remodeled it according to their needs. Downstairs, they created the big open workspaces they needed for the flower business. Upstairs, they eventually renovated two apartments: a one-bedroom and a studio. Luisa now lived in the one-bedroom apartment, but the studio served other purposes. It was a useful place for discussions with big clients, like the owners of the Piedmont

is  Th

Julio's Flower Shop – a place where beauty inspires more beauty

Pedro, Beatriz and Luisa's picture appeared in the Times Journal.

Hotel. However, it was also a place for the family and the staff to have a little privacy. "If we're spending most of our lives at *Julio's Flower Shop*," declared Beatriz, "We'll need some sort of refuge." And that's exactly what it was.

The walls in the studio were painted a light mango color. The arched doorway was outlined in turquoise blue. A side window, looking out on a tall jacaranda tree, was trimmed in colorful Mexican ceramic tiles. The room contained a long mahogany table that gleamed under the wrought-iron light fixture hanging from the ceiling. It was also furnished with a dark green antique sofa, a hand-painted cabinet, and a beautiful silver mirror on the wall. Whether it served as a conference room, a dining room, or an office, everyone loved the studio. A photo of Pedro, Beatriz, and Luisa taken there had also appeared in the *Times Journal* article last month. They all posed behind a huge vase of calla lilies on the table. The caption under the photo read: "*Julio's Flower Shop—a place where beauty inspires more beauty.*"

Beatriz emerged from the studio several minutes later. She looked perfectly satisfied when she found Luisa downstairs. "I just had a very nice conversation with Mrs. Brooks," she said. "Everything is fine. She and her daughter will be here tomorrow at 2:00p.m."

"Dreadful woman, isn't she?" said Luisa, tying a bunch of red tulips together.

"Not to me," said Beatriz. "In fact, she was surprisingly courteous*. You forgot to mention that you saved her life last night. What a miracle, *mija*! I'm so proud of you!"

"Well," said Luisa. "She certainly took the joy out of it."

"Luisa," said Beatriz. "I think you're exaggerating things a bit. On the telephone, I didn't hear the monster you've described. I'm actually looking forward to meeting her and her daughter. Anyway, someone named Ryan is driving them down here. Is he their chauffeur*?"

"Perhaps he is now," said Luisa, trying not to meet her mother's eyes. "He used to be their rose gardener. Next he might be required to carry them on his back through the streets. I'm sure they won't want to get their shoes dirty by walking in this neighborhood."

Beatriz cut another piece of ribbon and handed it to Luisa. "Well, she seemed nice enough to me," said Beatriz. "By the way, she asked if you would be at the meeting. It sounds like she's quite fond of you."

"Mamá, please understand that I will be nowhere near the shop at that time. I'll help Armando with the deliveries. If he doesn't need me, then I'll hide somewhere until they're gone. But I won't watch as Mrs. Brooks browbeats* you—

and she will. I'm pretty sure that she has a thing against Mexican-Americans."

"You underestimate me, Luisa," said Beatriz. "I've been in this world—and in this business—for a long time. I can take care of myself. I'm actually more worried about *you*."

"What are you talking about Mamá?" asked Luisa, defensively.

"You can't judge Mrs. Brooks on one or two awkward meetings, *mija*. You formed a bad opinion of her too quickly. Don't forget that this woman is helping to support *Julio's Flower Shop*. No one knows what she's been through in life— or what she's going through now. But there is something you should know: first impressions can be completely wrong."

❧ Chapter 12 ❧

Luisa Surprised

The next day, Luisa shared the afternoon deliveries with Armando. Luisa rarely made deliveries anymore, but today she actually looked forward to them. She had ten floral arrangements to transport: four to City Hospital, three to private residences, one to a retirement community, one to a downtown bank, and one to a funeral home. Before carefully loading the arrangements into the van, Luisa made sure that the personal-message cards matched their intended recipients. The mistake she made years ago still embarrassed her. She would be horrified if the bank clerk received "Rest in peace, dear Uncle Henry," or if the recently deceased* Uncle Henry received "Congratulations to our Employee of the Month!" Luisa winced* at the possibility and thoroughly checked them all again.

At 1:30p.m., Luisa jumped into the van with her half of the outgoing floral arrangements. Of course, she wanted to avoid the 2:00p.m. meeting with Mrs. Brooks, but it was a nice change in her routine, too. Delivering flowers was one of the more rewarding aspects of this job. People were always happy to receive flowers, and it was a joy to see their reactions. Besides, Luisa was determined to model hard work at every level of the business. She didn't want her employees to think that she was above going out on deliveries or sweeping the floor.

Luisa drove south on the highway toward City Hospital. She assumed that Mrs. Brooks and Sarah had arrived— thanks to Ryan—for their meeting with her mother. Would Ryan be allowed to enter the shop or would he be forced to wait in the car? "Hopefully," thought Luisa, bitterly, "Mrs. Brooks will let Ryan roll down the windows for a little fresh air." Her face suddenly felt very warm. She tried hard not to think about Ryan. "Don't think about him anymore!" she told herself, sternly*. "He isn't for you!" After all, Luisa could never respect a man who put up with that kind of treatment. Everyone needed to make a living, but there were other jobs in this city for gardeners and struggling business owners. She thought that Ryan should show some courage and find one.

Luisa turned up the radio in the van and tried to think about other things. But her thoughts soon returned to the clients from Oak Hills. She pictured her mother leading Mrs. Brooks and Sarah upstairs to the studio. It was funny to imagine Mrs. Brooks in the mango-colored room, away from her white marble floors and crystal chandelier. In that small area, would it be possible for Mrs. Brooks to accurately describe *cascading** floral arrangements? Her mother would probably need to shield her face from the dramatic arm circles. The idea made Luisa laugh out loud.

Earlier that morning, Beatriz had carried several grocery bags into the shop. Luisa suspected that they included some kind of refreshments for her clients. Beatriz would certainly offer them some coffee or tea, and perhaps some pastries. Luisa wondered if her mother had stopped at the Mexican bakery just three blocks from the shop. Then she thought again. Mrs. Brooks might be offended at the sight of *pan dulce*, so Beatriz probably went to the fancier, and much more expensive, one on 7th Avenue. As Beatriz hurried upstairs with her shopping bags, Luisa smiled mischievously* and said, "Just don't offer Mrs. Brooks any peppermint candies, Mamá. She might take it the wrong way."

Luisa's stomach growled just thinking about food. In her hurry to leave the shop on time she had missed eating lunch today. "Well," she thought, "I'll get back by 4:00 p.m. or so. Mrs. Brooks and the others will be long gone. Hopefully, Mamá will have something in one of those bags for me."

For the next two hours, Luisa traveled around the city and carried out her deliveries. It was wonderful to see that the flowers from *Julio's Flower Shop* brought happiness to so many people. "Lovely!" said a patient in the hospital, making room on her nightstand for a gorgeous spring arrangement. "I feel better already."

"Lovely! I feel better already."

Later, a woman was delighted when Luisa appeared on her doorstep with a purple and white iris bouquet. "My *favorite* flowers! Oh, that man!" she said, emotionally. "I've just changed the locks on my house, but after this, I might make him a new key. How sweet! Thank you!"

"You're welcome," said Luisa cheerfully. "Enjoy your flowers."

It was nearly 4:00 p.m. when Luisa finally returned to the shop. Emma was rearranging the shelves in the refrigerated case, and Katya was making the schedule for tomorrow's deliveries. Luisa decided not to interrupt them. She headed straight upstairs to find something to eat. As she climbed the steps to the landing between the two apartments, she smelled something wonderful. She heard her mother's voice coming from the studio. Was she talking to Papá? Had *Tía* Teresa or one of her brothers stopped by? Luisa opened the door to the studio. She stared inside but could not take a step past the doorway. She thought she must be dreaming.

❧ Chapter 13 ❧

Dinner with Mrs. Brooks

Mrs. Brooks and Sarah were both sitting at the mahogany table. Although they weren't quite eating out of her mother's palm, they were definitely about to eat from her favorite blue and white dishes. "You look like you've just seen a ghost, *mija*," said her mother. "Come and sit down with Mrs. Brooks and Sarah."

"Maybe she thinks I am a ghost," said Mrs. Brooks. "But I assure you that I'm still here, young lady—body and soul. In fact, I've never felt better. Miss Sánchez, you never told me about your delightful mother!"

"Oh, yes, we've had the most wonderful afternoon up here," added Sarah, rising from her seat and hugging Luisa warmly. "Your mother told us that you were very busy today, but she's taken excellent care of us. We've decided on all of the flowers—and my mother and I are still speaking to each other! So, Luisa, in addition to the miracle you performed the other night, there has clearly been another one today." Luisa remained motionless in the doorway, still unable to speak. She could not imagine a more unlikely scene than this one.

"Sit!" demanded Mrs. Brooks, pointing to a chair across from hers. "Your mother has gone to the trouble of preparing this lovely meal. I must say that it looks and smells perfectly divine. But we refuse to eat it in front of you." Luisa looked longingly at the pan of *enchiladas* with *tomatillo salsa*.

"I don't know," said Luisa, finally able to produce some words, "I should probably get back to the shop. I've been gone for a long time. They may need my help down there."

"Please sit down and enjoy our company," said Beatriz. "I just checked on them downstairs. Emma assures me that everything is under control."

"Of course it is," said Mrs. Brooks, as if she knew everything there was to know about their flower business. "Now, come here and eat—at once!" Luisa reluctantly sat down in the chair across from Mrs. Brooks. Her mother put a glass of *agua de Jamaica*, hibiscus-flower tea, in front of her. Even though Luisa had resolved never to speak to Mrs. Brooks again, she found it impossible to disobey her. Mrs. Brooks seemed to have a strange power over people. If she told them to sit, they sat. If she told them to eat, they ate. If she told them to get out of her house, they got out. It was simply impossible to argue with her.

Luisa saw that her mother was also very skilled in getting her own way. Beatriz was a brilliant salesperson. She probably sold Mrs. Brooks floral arrangements that were *cascading* from the sky. Luisa couldn't wait to hear the estimated flower bill for Sarah's wedding. The price tag for this one-day event could set a record for *Julio's Flower Shop*. However, Beatriz's methods of getting what she wanted were very different. Unlike Mrs. Brooks, Beatriz didn't bark out orders. She didn't frighten people with her terrible manners and constant irritability. Her mother lived by another expression: *You can catch more flies with honey than with vinegar*. And, judging by the results in this room, this was certainly true. Luisa noticed the sample bridal bouquet that her mother had put together for Sarah. The excited bride-to-be still clutched it in her hand. Beatriz had won these clients over with her charm, attentiveness, and delicious food.

Beatriz served her *enchiladas* with rice and *ensalada de col*. When she finally sat down, everyone began to eat. Luisa hadn't eaten since that morning, so the food tasted especially good. For a few minutes, everyone sat quietly and enjoyed the flavors of the wonderful meal. Luisa was halfway through her *enchilada* when she looked up and saw something shocking: Mrs. Brooks was crying. Immediately, Luisa was alarmed. And in spite of her resentment* toward Mrs. Brooks, once again Luisa jumped out of her chair and ran to her side. "Are you all right?" she asked, ready to do the Heimlich Maneuver again. Mrs. Brooks nodded her head.

"Yes, I'm fine," she answered. "It's just the food."

"Is it too spicy for you?" asked Beatriz. "I'll give you an *enchilada* without the *salsa*. Take a drink, Mrs. Brooks. Don't worry. It'll only take a moment," she said, getting out of her chair. "Maybe you're not used to Mexican food."

"On the contrary," said Mrs. Brooks. "Please don't get up. The food is wonderful. Sorry about the tears. I'm just a little emotional. That's all."

"Of course you are," said Beatriz, patting Mrs. Brooks tenderly on the shoulder. "Your daughter is getting married. I'll cry, too, when Luisa walks down the aisle someday."

"That isn't it," said Mrs. Brooks, wiping her eyes with a napkin. "I used to eat a lot of Mexican food, once upon a time. This food is just bringing back a lot of…memories."

❧ Chapter 14 ☙

A Terrible Shock

Mrs. Brooks dried her tears, blew her nose, and abruptly changed the subject. She insisted that Sarah tell Luisa all about their flower choices for the wedding. Sarah, however, was completely focused on the food. "This meal is amazing, Mrs. Sánchez. Without a doubt, this is the *best* Mexican food I've ever had," she said, gladly accepting a second *enchilada* from Beatriz. "Mom, wouldn't it make sense to have Mexican food at the wedding? This tastes so much better than the menu we've selected. No one really likes caviar and all of that fussy stuff." Luisa thought that Sarah's suggestion might cause another choking episode, but Mrs. Brooks seemed to actually consider it.

"Well, Sarah," she said. "It's one thing for Mrs. Sánchez to prepare a meal for four people. It's quite another to feed three hundred."

"My sister can do it," said Beatriz, instantly. "She has prepared food for countless events. She's a professional caterer." Luisa really couldn't believe her mother's nerve. Yes, she had seen *Tía* Teresa cook for several big parties over the years. Luisa agreed that her aunt was an excellent cook. But she doubted that *Tía* Teresa could meet the expectations of Mrs. Brooks on her daughter's wedding day.

"Mamá," said Luisa, "did you hear her? There will be *three hundred* guests at the wedding!"

"Teresa can have her staff assist her," said her mother, giving Luisa a serious look that told her to be silent. "I'll give you my sister's telephone number," Beatriz said to Mrs. Brooks, "and you can talk. Yes, it's true. Why serve caviar

47

when you can impress your guests with *ceviche*," she said, matter-of-factly. "In my opinion, it does taste much better."

Soon after they finished their delicious meal, Mrs. Brooks stood up and announced that they needed to go. "Call Ryan," she said to Sarah, abruptly. Luisa had, in fact, wondered about Ryan. She hoped that he hadn't been waiting in the car for over three hours.

"Do you mind if I call him from here, Mrs. Sánchez? Ryan is with some relatives now. They live near here—just over on 31st Street."

"Of course she doesn't mind," said Mrs. Brooks, not waiting for a response. "Call him this instant. We need to get back. If he doesn't pick up, go outside and whistle for him." Although Luisa had thoroughly enjoyed her meal, she now felt sickened. *Whistle for him?* Wasn't that how people called their dogs? Mrs. Brooks was certainly an enigma*. For the past few minutes, she had been almost tolerable. But now, Luisa absolutely detested her. She didn't care if this wedding generated a fortune for her family. They could swallow their pride and run up to Oak Hills with their flowers and *enchiladas*. Luisa wanted no part of it. She would do *almost* anything for *Julio's Flower Shop*, but she was determined never to lift a finger for Amanda Brooks.

Luisa accompanied the group downstairs. Beatriz and Mrs. Brooks chatted amiably, while Luisa pretended to be interested in Sarah's bridal bouquet. As the women talked, Luisa saw a car pull up to the curb. Sarah turned around and saw it too. "Ryan's here, Mom," she said.

"It's about time," sighed Mrs. Brooks.

"Oh, would you like me to make him a plate?" asked Beatriz. "I have a few more *enchiladas*."

"Oh, no. That isn't necessary," said Mrs. Brooks. "I'm sure Ryan had a little something with those people. He'll be just fine. If he gets hungry later, we'll toss* him a scrap outside."

"*Toss him a scrap outside?*" Luisa muttered in disbelief. She imagined Ryan scratching at the front door like a poor little dog. Then she pictured Mrs. Brooks throwing a half-eaten sandwich toward the rose garden.

Despite her affection for Mexican food, Mrs. Brooks clearly felt another way about actual Mexicans. To her, they were just peons*. Still, Luisa was curious as to why Mrs. Brooks bothered to be polite to her mother. She suspected the reason to be financial. The economy was bad, and it had probably affected Mrs. Brooks, too. Naturally, the services provided by the Sánchez family were going to be less expensive than the fancy florists and caterers in Oak Hills. Luisa's relatives were doing Mrs. Brooks a huge favor. But once the wedding was over, her mother would be treated with the same disrespect.

Luisa fought a sudden urge to push Mrs. Brooks right out the front door. She had intended to wait in the shop, but was now compelled to follow everyone outside. She watched as Ryan dutifully got out of the car. He looked very handsome in his long-sleeved shirt and black pants. He even introduced himself to her mother: "Hi, I'm Ryan Soto," he said. "It's a pleasure to meet you, Mrs. Sánchez." Then he opened the passenger doors for Mrs. Brooks and Sarah.

"At your service, Ma'am," he said to Mrs. Brooks with a smile. Then his eyes met Luisa's. "Hi, Luisa," he said, smiling broadly. "Nice to see you again."

"You're late," said Mrs. Brooks with annoyance. "What took you so long?"

"I was enjoying being with my family. Sometimes it takes a while to say good-bye."

"You're ridiculous," she said. "Now drive us home," she ordered, getting into the back seat. Sarah got into the front seat and rolled down her window. She thanked Beatriz again for her time and hospitality. Meanwhile, Luisa stepped toward Ryan on the sidewalk. She looked earnestly into his kind eyes.

"I think you have my phone number," she said, very quietly. "Can you please call me after you drop them off? I really need to talk to you."

❧ Chapter 15 ❧

A Call from Ryan

When *Julio's Flower Shop* closed at 6:00p.m., Luisa and Emma were alone inside. "Don't worry about the blinds," Luisa said, as Emma began to lower them over the windows. "I can close them. Please go home and enjoy your dinner," she added, handing Emma some *enchiladas* on a covered paper plate.

"Thanks!" said Emma. "Are you sure?"

"Positive," said Luisa. "Everything is under control here. I'll be going upstairs to my apartment in just a little while." Luisa followed Emma to the front door.

"Okay," said Emma. "I'll see you tomorrow, then."

"Great. And thanks so much for your help today. Have a good evening," said Luisa, locking the door behind Emma. She looked up at the clock. Hopefully, Mrs. Brooks and Sarah were home by now, and Ryan would be calling soon. Luisa was glad that the shop was empty. She definitely didn't want anyone to overhear this telephone conversation. Luisa finished closing the blinds and then picked up the broom. As she swept up the flower petals, leaves, and stems that had fallen onto the floor, she planned exactly what she needed to say.

Surely, Luisa and Ryan would both agree that Mrs. Brooks was an evil human being. Luisa didn't need to draw attention to her many character flaws and examples of cruelty. Ryan obviously suffered from them day and night. They also didn't need to gossip about Mrs. Brooks or call her names—although Luisa could think of several that she rightly deserved. Nevertheless, the real issue, Luisa believed, was not Mrs. Brooks. Sadly, there were plenty of people like her in the world. Luisa's greater concern was for Ryan. She desperately wanted to know why he allowed himself to be abused by her.

Luisa was pouring the contents of her dustpan into the trash when the telephone rang. It was Ryan. "Hi, Luisa!" he said warmly when she picked up the phone in the shop. "It was great to see you briefly this afternoon."

"Hi, Ryan," said Luisa, more guardedly. "Yes, nice to see you, too."

"I was just wondering how long you've worked for Mrs. Brooks."

"I know you're very busy, but I'd really like to arrange a time to go out for lunch or dinner—or something. I have some family in your part of town, so I'm down there a lot. Is there a day and time that works for you?"

Luisa felt uneasy. This was not the conversation that she wanted to have. For a moment, she didn't say anything, and Ryan felt very uncomfortable.

"Or you can check your calendar and get back to me," he said, awkwardly. "You asked me to call you tonight, so I thought that…"

"No," said Luisa. "I mean, *yes*, I did ask you to call. I was just wondering, uh…" Luisa was losing her courage. The words she had rehearsed were difficult to say. "Uh, I was just wondering how long you've worked for Mrs. Brooks."

"Is that why you wanted me to call?" Ryan asked. "You wanted to know how long I've worked for Mrs. Brooks? That's kind of an odd question." He laughed a little uneasily. "Well," he said, "it's been a long time, I suppose."

"And what do you think of the way she treats you?" Luisa asked. This time she didn't wait for a response. "I mean, to me, it doesn't appear like she respects you very much. She orders you around like a servant. You can't set foot in her house. She seems, well, very harsh and frankly, I don't know why you stand for it." There. Luisa had, more or less, said what she wanted to say. Ryan's response, however, was not at all what she expected. He burst out laughing.

"Luisa," he said. "Yes, I know that my employer can be a bit, well, abrasive*. But didn't your family just get a rather large flower contract from her? Truly, she can't be all bad."

"Look, Ryan," said Luisa, seriously. "I am actually no longer managing the account for this wedding. My parents, however, are still the owners of this business. And they are very grateful to have Mrs. Brooks as their client. But I've noticed from the beginning that she is mean and unfair to you. I'm sorry, but from one Latino to another, I don't understand why you work for her. It's quite clear that she dislikes Mexicans. Have you thought about reporting her for violating anti-discrimination laws? Or have you at least thought about looking for another job away from that racist…"

"Whoa, Luisa!" Ryan exclaimed. "Please don't say another word." Ryan took a deep breath. "Look, I sincerely appreciate your concern for me. But you're wrong about Mrs. Brooks. Believe me, I'm treated very fairly. And she's definitely *not* a racist. But can we please not talk about this right now? Instead, let's figure out a day and time to, maybe, go out somewhere—if you still want to." Obviously, this was a sensitive subject for Ryan. And because he pretended not to see the truth, Luisa felt sorrier for him than before.

"Okay," said Luisa, realizing that the topic was a painful one. Still, she could not end the conversation and say good-bye. She looked at her calendar. "I'm doing another wedding on Saturday, but I'll be free after that. Let's meet at the shop at 6:30p.m."

Chapter 16

First Date

Luisa slipped on her shoes in the apartment above *Julio's Flower Shop*. Tonight was her date with Ryan. She remained very surprised by their recent telephone conversation. Obviously, she had planned for things to go very differently. Luisa simply wanted to point out that Ryan worked for a tyrant. Then she wanted to offer some well-meaning advice, hang up, and forget about him forever. She never expected Ryan to defend Mrs. Brooks. Sadly, his reaction made him seem pathetic and weak. Even stranger, Ryan immediately changed the subject and asked her out. And, against her better judgment, Luisa had agreed. There was something about Ryan's voice—and his picture in her mind—that also made her weak. Instead of hanging up and forgetting about him forever, she now nervously smoothed down her hair and applied a pretty shade of pink lipstick. Apparently, they were both cowards*.

Luisa looked at the clock. In a few minutes, Ryan would be coming into the shop. She walked down the stairs and decided to wait for him there. Once again, she was happy that everyone had already left. She didn't want her private life to be exposed, although everyone would enjoy the show. She could imagine Emma playfully removing the petals of a daisy: "*He loves me…He loves me not…He loves me…*" Even worse would be her own mother's reaction: "Not the gardener, *mija*! Please let Arturo find you a nice young man—with some money—at the law firm."

Soon, there was a quiet knock on the front door of *Julio's Flower Shop*. It was Ryan. Luisa looked at his handsome face

55

through the glass. He was dressed very nicely in a blue jacket and brown pants. "Well," she thought to herself, "he may be somewhat spineless, but he is, without a doubt, the best-looking man in the entire world." Luisa unlocked the door. Ryan entered the shop and hugged her gently.

"Hi, Luisa," he said. "You look beautiful. It's great to see you." Luisa felt her knees go weak. In spite of her resolve*, it was impossible not to like Ryan.

"You, too, Ryan," she said. "Please come in. Would you like to see the shop?"

"Sure," he said. "I'd love to." Luisa showed him the different areas where employees worked and floral arrangements were made.

"Wow!" said Ryan. "This is very impressive. I've actually been in here once before, but I didn't realize this place was so big."

"You've been in *Julio's Flower Shop* before?" asked Luisa with surprise. "When?"

"It was probably about three months ago," said Ryan. "I bought some purple dahlias for my aunt's birthday. You didn't wait on me, though. It was another woman."

"It was probably Emma," said Luisa, smiling at the thought of Ryan as a customer.

"But," he continued, "I did notice a woman standing over there at the worktable. She was thoroughly engaged in creating a very pretty floral arrangement. It was almost as pretty as she was. Well, not *was*, but *is*, because now I know that *she* was really *you*." Luisa felt the warmness in her face again.

"Oh, Ryan." she said, "That's a very sweet thing to say."

"Or it could have been your mother," Ryan said, scratching his head. "You know, she's very beautiful, too."

His comment made them both laugh out loud. "Later," Ryan added, "I happened to read the article about your family in the *Times Journal*. Then, as luck would have it, Mrs. Brooks needed a florist for Sarah's wedding. And the next thing I knew, you appeared at the estate in Oak Hills."

"Well, how about that?" said Luisa, amused by this funny chain of events. "Maybe something good did come of that whole experience."

"It certainly did for me," said Ryan, reaching for Luisa's hand. "I guess we should go to the restaurant now. Are you hungry?"

"I'm starving," said Luisa, thoroughly enjoying the feeling of his strong hand around hers. But the truth was, Luisa was no longer hungry at all. With all of the butterflies in her stomach, she couldn't eat a thing.

❧ **Chapter 17** ❧

New Love

For the following two months, Luisa dated Ryan. And in her entire twenty-five years of life, she had never, ever been so happy. Apart from Ryan continuing, inexplicably*, to work for Mrs. Brooks, he appeared to have absolutely no faults. She enjoyed every moment of his company. And on the days and evenings when they were too busy—or too tired—to see each other, they talked for a long time on the telephone.

During one of their first late-night phone conversations, Luisa learned that Ryan's immediate family lived somewhere up north. He seemed to have a great affection for them. Ryan laughingly recounted a story of their disappointment when he chose to major in landscape architecture at the university. His mother, in particular, never understood his fascination with horticulture*. "You know how mothers are," said Ryan with amusement. "They're imagining a doctor or a lawyer—not some weird kid who is grafting rose cuttings in the front yard."

During their time together, Luisa and Ryan often liked to go out for dinner or to the movies. They sometimes visited Ryan's aunt, uncle, and cousins on 31st Street. And, as luck would have it, Luisa really enjoyed their company. Ryan, too, had attended a couple of the Sunday gatherings in the Sánchez home. And because Ryan was Ryan, everyone immediately liked him. Beatriz was, perhaps, a little more reluctant to approve of him. After all, she had bigger dreams for her daughter. It was only natural that she worried about Ryan ever making the money that he needed to help support her daughter—and perhaps a family someday. "Isn't he wonderful, Mamá?" said Luisa adoringly, as Ryan chatted with *Tia* Teresa in the next room.

"Yes," said Beatriz, wiping her hands on a kitchen towel, "the gardener is a very nice boy."

"The *landscape architect*, Mamá," Luisa reminded her. "And college-educated, don't forget."

"Yes, but still digging in the dirt full time," said Beatriz, "for minimum-wage, probably." Luisa folded her arms and looked away from her mother. "*Mija*, money is very important in a relationship. I'm warning you that when the hearts-and-flowers stage of a romance is over, resentment can build. Please *look before you leap*."

Luisa's father, on the other hand, completely approved of Ryan. He also spoke to him encouragingly about his work. "Maybe things are a little slow for you right now, but that will change." One Sunday, Pedro even suggested a possible business opportunity for *Soto Landscape Architecture*. "Several shopkeepers on 29th Street have discussed making some outside improvements," he said. "For one thing, we all need better landscaping in front of our stores. In my opinion, it would be a very smart investment. Undoubtedly, an appealing street will bring more customers into the neighborhood. What do you think, Ryan?"

"It would be a dream to manage a project like that," said Ryan enthusiastically.

"Well," said Pedro, patting Ryan's shoulder, "Why don't you write up a proposal for our next storeowners and tenants meeting? It's in about three weeks. I have a feeling that they'll really like the idea."

"Oh, Papá!" said Luisa, "I can't think of a better person to handle a job like that." Ryan was beaming.

"I can't wait to share my thoughts with them," said Ryan. "I'll get started on a proposal and some drawings as soon as I can." Luisa felt very excited and squeezed Ryan's arm affectionately. This could be a huge professional break for him. A beautification project along 29th Street could quickly lead to other work. Success in Ryan's professional life would give him the confidence to leave his degrading position in Oak Hills, where he worked—and lived—like a dog. In truth, Luisa had never actually seen the caretaker's cottage where he slept on the estate. According to Ryan, it was relatively small. Of course, Luisa understood that the housing included in his job was beneficial. Nevertheless, she pictured him crawling into a tiny doghouse every night. And she was sure that Mrs. Brooks didn't pay him much beyond that.

For the most part, Luisa and Ryan tried not to discuss his work in Oak Hills. The subject of Mrs. Brooks always led to tension between them, so it was better not to mention her. However, Ryan had become increasingly busy lately. Sarah's wedding was at the weekend and there was a lot of work to be done. On the Thursday evening before the wedding, they met at a downtown restaurant. Ryan proudly gave Luisa a beautiful red rose from the garden. "This is for you, lovely Luisa. I wish you would come up again for a visit. The roses are blooming, and it's just incredible," he said, showing her a photo on his phone. "The picture doesn't do it justice."

"I'm sure it doesn't," said Luisa, with admiration, "and I'd love to see the whole garden. But I would hate to run into Mrs. Brooks. You know that I can't stand her."

"Yeah, right," said Ryan, looking down at his salad.

"And be careful about removing her property," said Luisa, smelling the rose. "Mrs. Brooks is the type to have you arrested."

❧ Chapter 18 ❧

Wedding Preparation

The day before the wedding in Oak Hills, *Julio's Flower Shop* was humming with activity. Pedro, Beatriz, Luisa, Katya, Emma, and Armando were all working non-stop on the account in Oak Hills. Because this wedding was so laborious, Luisa had no choice but to help out, too. "This effort is only for Sarah," she reasoned to herself, as she lifted up a heavy bucket of lilies in water. "*She* is actually a very nice young woman and *the complete opposite of her mother.*"

The next morning, the telephone woke Luisa up at 5:00a.m. "We need your support, *mija!*" begged her mother. "Katya's son has the flu and she can't leave him. Please help us with the wedding in Oak Hills! We're trying to recruit* a few more people, but most of them have gone to help *Tia* Teresa in the kitchen. Your father is on the other phone asking your cousins, Alma and Elsa, for help. *Ay, we've bitten off more than we can chew!*"

"Calm down, Mamá," said Luisa, reassuringly. She had been afraid that something like this would happen. "You know that I'll help you." Luisa heard her mother sigh with relief on the other end. She had worried about her parents handling this event without her. This was not a typical wedding for *Julio's Flower Shop.* There were very elaborate plans for both flowers and food. The entire Sanchez family was assuming a huge responsibility. And, of course, this concerned Luisa, too.

"Please wear something nice to the wedding," said Beatriz. "As the owners of this business, your father and I are dressing up, too. No one will ask you to carry buckets, climb ladders, or get dirty. Basically, we'll just need you as a coordinator. Your job will be to direct the less experienced staff. They need to be told exactly what to do. Bless you, *mija*."

"Mamá," said Luisa, yawning. "What time is this wedding? I've forgotten."

"The wedding ceremony in the rose garden isn't until 4:00p.m. Then the reception in the big tent goes from 5:00p.m. or so—until late. So, we'll be at the shop in an hour to get everything organized. I'm thinking that we'll need to be up in Oak Hills no later than 1:00p.m. Of course, we can't put the flowers out too early or they will wilt—as you know. *Ay*, there's a lot of work to do!"

Luisa crawled out of bed and rubbed her eyes. Somehow, she knew all along that she would get mixed up in this wedding. Luisa had planned to stay in the shop today. But it made more sense to keep Emma there, now that Katya wasn't available. Luisa wasn't angry with Katya. Children sometimes got sick at inconvenient times. It was Luisa's duty, as the manager of this business, to offer assistance. She had to forget about Beatriz's promise not to involve her. "Just focus on helping *Julio's Flower Shop*," Luisa thought to herself, "and not on that ogre, Mrs. Brooks."

Luisa forced herself to eat a piece of toast and drink a glass of juice. Then she opened her closet and considered what to wear. She picked out a pretty yellow dress. She had only worn it once before, when her parents were honored at a local business luncheon. It was dressy enough, but not too uncomfortable. "Well, at least I can see the rose garden," Luisa thought, trying to look at her predicament* positively. "Ryan will like that I can finally see the results of all of his hard work. And I'll just stay far, far away from Mrs. Brooks."

As promised, Luisa's parents appeared with their extra workers early in the morning. Countless bouquets and arrangements were prepared and kept in the cooler. Other flowers were put into large buckets, to be assembled once they got to Oak Hills. Finally, everything was loaded into four refrigerated vans.

She picked out a pretty yellow dress for the wedding.

At 11:00a.m., Luisa ran upstairs to get ready for the wedding. Once she was dressed, she ran back downstairs and got into the passenger side of her father's van. Then they headed north to Oak Hills with the others. On the way, Luisa received a funny text message from Ryan. It said: "Beautiful day for a wedding. Roses stunning. Mrs. Brooks on a rampage*." Luisa laughed out loud. She decided not to respond. He could be pleasantly surprised by her unexpected appearance. And perhaps, with Mrs. Brooks so distracted, they could sneak into her house and get something delicious from *Tia* Teresa in the kitchen. Then they could secretly eat some messy Mexican food *inside* Mrs. Brooks' fancy house. Luisa was delighted by the idea.

By 1:00p.m., the vans carrying flowers to the wedding passed through the large iron gate. "How do you like the Brooks Mansion, Papá?" asked Luisa. Her father was speechless for a moment before answering.

"Unbelievable," said her father. "It's always surprising to *see how the other half lives*."

Soon, the team of employees, relatives, and friends began following Luisa's specific instructions. Then Sarah ran outside to meet them. Although she was wearing a beautiful bridal veil, she was still dressed in her blouse and jeans. "Oh, Luisa, Beatriz, and…everyone. You're here! I'm so excited! Wow!" she said, as people began unloading flowers from the van. "Everything looks so pretty! I'm so grateful to you. This is just the happiest day of my life!" Meanwhile, Mrs. Brooks came tearing out of the house in her metallic-gold formal gown. Luisa couldn't believe how fast she could run, even in her high heels. She fought a very strong urge to laugh.

"Oh, Mrs. Brooks," said Beatriz, as she approached them. "You look just lovely!"

"Sarah," Mrs. Brooks snapped, ignoring the compliment. "Get into the house *at once* and put on your dress. The photographers are here! They want to get some family pictures before the ceremony. Now," she said, her eyes darting around the rose garden, "where on earth is Ryan?"

"Do you really need him?" asked Luisa, bravely. She wondered why Mrs. Brooks had to have Ryan at that very moment.

"Obviously," said Mrs. Brooks. Luisa frowned. She didn't understand. She suspected that Mrs. Brooks was going to give him some demoralizing* task, like smoothing out the dirt under their feet—with his bare hands.

"You need Ryan…the *gardener*…right now…for your pictures?" persisted Luisa, feeling her anger rising. Beatriz put her arm on her daughter's shoulder in an effort to calm her.

"My dear," said Mrs. Brooks with exasperation. "I sincerely wish you would stop calling him the *gardener*. If you didn't already know, Ryan is my *son*!"

❧ Chapter 19 ❧
A Shocking Revelation

As Mrs. Brooks ran back to the house, Luisa stared at Beatriz with her mouth wide open. She was thunderstruck*. Impossible! Perhaps she hadn't heard Mrs. Brooks correctly. Or perhaps Mrs. Brooks was joking. Or perhaps this was all a dream. Luisa pinched herself on the arm to see if it was a dream. But the pinch hurt. So it was true: Ryan Soto, her boyfriend of over two months, was Mrs. Brooks' *son*. Why hadn't Ryan told her before? Luisa shuddered to think of the horrible things she had said about his mother.

Beatriz saw that her daughter was in a complete state of shock. She gently took hold of Luisa's hand and led her to the side of one of the vans. "Forget what I said about your gardener," Beatriz said, cheerfully. "I now like Ryan very much. This relationship has my blessing, *mija*." Luisa instantly broke free of her mother's hand.

"We have a lot of work to do, Mamá," Luisa said, without emotion. First, she told the workers exactly how to position the *cascading* floral arrangements on the long head table. Next, she pointed out all the flowers that belonged on the guest tables. Then she explained where to hang even more flowers among the overhead lights in the tent. Finally, she gave directions for the hundreds of floating candles to be used after sunset. There was nothing *simple* about the appearance of this wedding. Mrs. Brooks got everything she wanted and—thanks to Beatriz—more.

Right now, Luisa had to bring the bouquets and boutonnieres to the members of the wedding party. They were needed immediately for the photos. Luisa opened one of the vans, picked up two large boxes, and carried them toward the mansion. She knocked lightly on the front door. After a moment, Ryan appeared. He was wearing a black tuxedo. And he had never looked more handsome. This time, however, it was Ryan who looked like he had seen a ghost. "What a surprise, Luisa!" he said, attempting to give her a kiss. "I didn't expect to see…you…here."

"I didn't expect to be here," said Luisa, sharply turning away from him so that his kiss landed on one of the boxes. "We were shorthanded, so I had to come. As you see, I have flowers for all the members of the wedding party. Would you kindly direct me to them?"

"Sure," said Ryan. "The women are all upstairs in Sarah's room, and the men are down here on the first floor."

"Great," said Luisa, coolly. "And I have a special corsage* for the mother of the bride. Do you know where I can find Mrs. Brooks?"

"Um, sure," said Ryan. "Or I can take it to her. I know that you're really busy." Just then, Mrs. Brooks appeared at the top of the stairs. She looked down at Luisa and Ryan.

"Is that you, Luisa?" she called. "Good timing. Everyone is dressed and ready for the pictures."

"Okay, I'll be right up, Mrs. Brooks." Then Luisa turned back to Ryan, who looked even paler than before. "It's interesting," she observed, "that you have such a big role in this wedding. I didn't think Mrs. Brooks would ask her *gardener* to wear a tuxedo. And here you are, standing in her home. I always thought that you weren't allowed inside." Luisa's sarcastic tone revealed that she knew the truth.

"Listen, Luisa," said Ryan. "I can explain…"

"Ryan," said Luisa. "You've had two months to explain. But I refuse to have this discussion now. This is a big day for

Sarah—and for your whole family. Let me just do my job, okay?"

Luisa didn't wait for a response from Ryan. She headed straight upstairs, trying not to cry. At the end of a long marble hallway, she found Sarah. The bride was now dressed in her stunning wedding gown and posing for a photographer. "Oh, my!" said Luisa emotionally, handing Sarah the bridal bouquet. "You look so beautiful!" Luisa was suddenly overcome. A little sob escaped from her mouth. It was all too much to handle. First, there was the crazy news about Ryan. Now, here was his lovely *sister* on her wedding day.

"Don't cry, Luisa!" begged Sarah. "You'll make me cry." She walked away from the photographer and gave Luisa a hug. "And I'll smear all of this makeup that I never wear." Luisa put her hand over her mouth.

"I'll stop," said Luisa, trying to regain her composure*. "Sorry. I'm just…so…happy for you." Luisa didn't want to share the real reason for her tears. She went into Sarah's bedroom and dutifully passed out the bouquets to the five bridesmaids. And last, she brought a special corsage to Mrs. Brooks.

"Thank you," said Mrs. Brooks, as Luisa carefully pinned it to her gown. "I'd very much like a photo of this young woman with me," she called to one of the photographers. "She saved my life, you know. We can't forget that." Luisa obediently posed with Mrs. Brooks and tried to smile. Then she walked downstairs and found the men getting ready. Ryan stood among them, but Luisa tried not to look at him.

"I have a special boutonniere* for the groom," she said, to no one in particular. "Is he here?" she asked, picking up the one with the red rose.

"*Sí, soy yo*," said a very excited young man, raising his hand.

"This day just keeps getting stranger," thought Luisa, pinning the red rose onto the happy young man's tuxedo. "And now I've seen everything. Sarah is marrying a Mexican."

❧ Chapter 20 ☙

Luisa's Reaction

By 3:30p.m., the flowers were all in place. Luisa was certain that Sarah, Mrs. Brooks, and everyone else would be satisfied. The floral arrangements were lavish*, but very tasteful. Luisa watched as Pedro proudly walked around and took photos for the website. Outside the tent, rows and rows of chairs were placed on each side of the walkway in the rose garden. Luisa paused for a moment to admire it. There were hundreds of rose bushes, all in bloom, in every imaginable color. It was a breathtaking sight. And Ryan was responsible for all of it. Luisa wished that she could give him the praise he deserved. But perhaps they were no longer a couple. After today's surprises, she was not sure about anything.

Luisa knew that the wedding guests would be arriving soon. Her two cousins, Alma and Elsa, were performing the last task—scattering bags of rose petals everywhere. Luisa picked up one of the bags and opened it. "I'll do the area around the head table," she offered. "I know just how they want it." So Luisa, her arms circling dramatically, began to scatter the whole area, table and floor, with rose petals. Once again, she felt overcome with emotion. Her father stood by with his camera and watched her. "Luisa," he said, quietly. "Your mother shared some interesting news with me about Ryan."

"Who could have imagined this, Papá?" asked Luisa, angrily throwing a handful of rose petals in no particular direction. "Well, if Ryan doesn't get that landscaping job on 29th Street, I suppose it isn't the end of the world. After all," she said, pointing outside to the Brooks Mansion, "it appears that he still has a roof over his head." Pedro put his arm around Luisa soothingly. "Really, Papá, I feel so upset by his dishonesty." Once again, she tried to fight back tears.

"Give him a chance to explain, Luisa," said Pedro. "These people have a different view of life. In a way, I understand their need for privacy." Just then, a figure came up behind them. She was breathing loudly. It was *Tia* Teresa.

"What?" she said, "Who needs privacy?"

"The Brooks family, probably," said Pedro, looking at her with surprise. "Where did you come from?"

"The kitchen," she said. "But I don't think they need that much privacy. My staff and I have been living in the main house for the past three days. Mrs. Brooks has a huge kitchen, equipped with a giant industrial stove and three refrigerators. It just made sense to prepare all of the food there. In the evenings, we've been roaming all over the place and having a great time with Amanda. It's very nice inside, isn't it Luisa?" Luisa was now inclined to laugh. *Tia* Teresa living in the Brooks Mansion was also unimaginable.

"Yeah," said Luisa. "It's pretty nice."

"Mrs. Brooks doesn't really mind people coming and going. She only gets upset when Ryan walks inside with his dirty boots. She *hates* that. It scratches up her white marble floors. But you never told us your big secret," she added, looking at Luisa. "When I heard that Ryan was her son, I almost fell over."

"So did I," Luisa agreed.

"Forget the lawyers and the engineers," *Tia* Teresa laughed. "You were right all along to stick with the handsome gardener."

Luisa looked outside of the tent toward the rose garden. A twelve-piece *mariachi* band had begun to play outside. Guests were arriving and being led to their seats. Meanwhile, all but one of the flower vans had left with the extra workers. Luisa, Beatriz, and Pedro took one last look around at the exquisite floral arrangements they had created. Then, satisfied that everything was perfect, they began to walk toward the van.

"Where do you think you're going?" boomed a voice behind them. The three of them turned around in surprise. Once again, Mrs. Brooks was running toward them. "You're not leaving, are you?" Pedro and Beatriz looked at her awkwardly, and Luisa looked at the ground—now adequately covered in rose petals.

"Is there something else we can do for you?" asked Pedro, looking up at the flowers hanging from the lights. "Is there a problem somewhere?"

"Yes, there is a problem," said Mrs. Brooks. "You're obviously getting ready to leave, and I insist that you join the other guests right now!"

"Well, Mrs. Brooks," said Luisa, politely, "It's not usual for your, uh, vendors, to stay for the event."

"Nonsense!" she said. "Besides, you're not *just* my vendors. Young lady, you once saved my life. And now, my son claims to be madly in love with you. So, you and your parents must join the other wedding guests right now." Luisa and her parents looked at each other.

"If you insist, Amanda," said Beatriz. "We would be honored to celebrate this happy occasion with you."

"Good," said Mrs. Brooks, tapping her foot to the *mariachi* music. "There's nothing more fun than a big Mexican wedding, is there?" Mrs. Brooks clapped her hands together and smiled. "Then it's all settled," she said, pointing to the chairs in the rose garden. "Now, sit!"

Chapter 21
Sarah's Wedding

Luisa, Beatriz and Pedro walked in the direction of the rose garden. Ryan immediately walked over to greet them. "I'm so glad you're staying," he said. "It means a lot to all of us."

"We're glad to be here, *mijo*," said Beatriz, reaching up and pinching his cheek affectionately. "And you look so handsome!" Luisa tried to maintain a blank expression, but it wasn't easy. Ryan offered Beatriz his arm and took them to three seats near the front. As they sat down, he leaned over and whispered in Luisa's ear. "I know that you must be very shocked by all of this. But please give me a chance to explain later." Then he walked back into the crowd of guests.

Shortly after 4:00 p.m., Ryan escorted his mother up the long walkway. Mrs. Brooks sat in the first seat on the left side of the front row. Then Ryan turned around, winked quickly at Luisa in the fifth row, and walked all the way back. Meanwhile, the groom and his five groomsmen appeared with the priest to await the procession. As the bridesmaids made their way down the walkway, *Tia* Teresa sat down next to Luisa and leaned over toward her. "Did you know that Ryan is walking Sarah down the aisle?" she asked, quietly. Luisa shook her head. "Sarah's father died two years ago," her aunt continued, "after a very long illness. He's the second husband Mrs. Brooks has lost. Poor thing! While it's true that she has all of this, that woman hasn't had an easy life. I wouldn't trade with her."

Luisa tried not to react, but tears began to stream down her face. Her show of emotion, however, was finally allowed. Many guests were crying as the *mariachis* played a stirring version of Pachelbel's Canon in D. Finally, Sarah and Ryan came down the walkway. Everyone stood up to show respect for the beautiful bride, escorted by her devoted brother. "And here we are," thought Luisa, "with their family and friends on a perfect day in a magnificent rose garden." Naturally, in addition to the glorious sounds of violins and guitars, there were the sounds of weeping and sniffling all around them. Luisa's tears didn't attract attention at all.

Everyone stood up to show respect for the beautiful bride.

The reception was a great success. Everyone loved the flowers. Mrs. Brooks introduced Pedro and Beatriz to several of her friends. "Oh, my daughter is getting married next year," said one. "What you've created here is just magical. Can I call you?" Pedro resisted the temptation to pass out business cards at every table, but he was sure that this event would generate more business for *Julio's Flower Shop* regardless.

The wedding feast was also a triumph. *Tia* Teresa and her staff created the most wonderful selection of foods: *ceviche, tamales, chiles rellenos, enchiladas, carne asada, tacos* and Mexican *paella*. There were delicious salads and beautiful arrangements of fruit and cheese. Also, Mrs. Brooks had decided to hire additional servers so that Teresa and her friends could enjoy the wedding. "You won't do another thing," she declared, after their third day in her home. "At the wedding, you will all be sitting or dancing—for your full pay." Mrs. Brooks gladly gave Teresa credit for the wonderful food. After dinner, she made a point of introducing Teresa to her friend, Darcy Blackwell.

"Our company is having our annual holiday party in December," said Mrs. Blackwell, shaking Teresa's hand, warmly. "Do you think you can cater it?"

"I'll need to look at my calendar," said Teresa, smiling, as Mrs. Blackwell reached for her card. "I'll check with my staff and get back to you."

"Thanks," she said. "I won't pick a date until you let me know when you're free."

Eventually, the bride and groom made their way to the table where the Sánchez Family was sitting. Sarah sincerely thanked them for the incredible flowers. Then she introduced them to Jaime Romero, her new husband. "Nice to meet you all," said Jaime, in perfect English.

"You, too!" said Beatriz. "And congratulations! You make such a lovely couple."

"Thank you," said Sarah, hugging Beatriz affectionately. "We really appreciate all that you've done to make this so special."

"So," said Beatriz. "I love a romantic story. Where did the two of you meet?" she asked.

"I met Jaime through our foundation," replied Sarah. "You see, twenty years ago, my mother started an organization to support high-achieving Latino students. She named it after her first husband, who died when Ryan was very young. It's called the *Alberto Soto Foundation*. Anyway, Jaime's company is a donor*, and we met at a fundraising event. I'm proud to say that we've given academic scholarships* to hundreds of deserving kids. Have you ever heard of it?"

"We have," said Luisa, feeling tears forming in her eyes once again. "Thanks to your foundation, my brothers and I went to college."

❧ Chapter 22 ❦
Ryan Explains Himself

Naturally, Ryan had many obligations to fulfill at the wedding. There were many guests to receive, and he wanted everyone to feel welcome. When the dancing began at around 9:00p.m., he finally had an opportunity to speak with Luisa. He walked over to the table and asked her to dance, and she willingly accepted.

Luisa no longer felt angry. How was it possible to feel bitterness toward the people who had helped pay her way through college? More than anything else, she felt foolish. As Ryan held her closely on the dance floor, she really had only one question for him: "Why didn't you tell me?" Ryan sighed and looked into her deep brown eyes.

"I had been meaning to tell you, Luisa," he said, carefully gliding her among the crowd of dancers. "But it seemed that every time we got on the subject of Mrs. Brooks, uh, my *mother,* you got very hostile*. I thought that later, when the wedding was over, I could reintroduce her to you—without flower arrangements, choking incidents, and dirty work boots getting in the way."

"I can understand that she was under a lot of stress, Ryan," said Luisa, feeling his strong arm around her waist. "But you could have explained her behavior to me a lot earlier. For example, you could have said: *'My mother has a fit when I wear my dirty work boots in the house.'* Instead, you gave me the impression that you weren't allowed inside, like some kind of second-class citizen."

"I never said that," said Ryan, stopping on the dance floor for a moment. "You made that assumption."

"Well, of course I did. Then, my initial bad impression of your mother became far worse. Until today, I believed that she mistreated you because of your blue-collar job and Latino ancestry. Obviously this was not the case, and I feel terrible about it now."

When the music stopped, Ryan led Luisa off the dance floor. They walked out of the tent, hand in hand, toward the moonlit rose garden.

"It was wrong of me, I suppose," said Ryan, "And I guess that I could have cleared this up a lot earlier. But, Luisa," he continued, gently touching one of the curls in her hair. "I was immediately attracted to you."

"And?" asked Luisa.

"Well, in some past relationships, my money was an issue. This house," he said, pointing to the Brooks Mansion, "was an issue. More often than not, women were interested in me because of what I had, not for what I was. Frankly, I wanted to see if you would like me if I were—just a gardener."

"I sort of get that," said Luisa, quietly. "But you kept me in the dark for two whole months! That's a long time, Ryan. I had nightmares about Mrs. Brooks *whistling for you* and *tossing you a scrap outside.*"

"Oh," chuckled Ryan, "that *whistle* is still a joke in our family. When I was eight, I insisted that my mother call me into the house with a special whistle." Ryan demonstrated it for Luisa. It sounded like an exotic birdcall. Luisa had to laugh. "It's true," said Ryan. "It took my mother months of practice before she learned it." Ryan shrugged his shoulders. "I knew that the image was upsetting to you," he said, "but she meant it to be funny."

"And to think," said Luisa, "night after night, I worried about you being abused by a tyrant and sleeping in a doghouse." Ryan had to laugh.

"No, my mother isn't a tyrant—most of the time. And she clearly gets along with Mexicans," Ryan said, pointing to his mother inside the tent with the guests. Wearing one of the *mariachi's* hats, Mrs. Brooks was now serenading* the bride and groom—in Spanish. "Hey, I'll bet you never knew that she could sing like that."

Luisa pulled herself away from Ryan and pinched herself again. "Ouch!" she said.

"What are you doing?" asked Ryan.

"Sorry," said Luisa. "But your mother singing with the *mariachis* may be the most unbelievable sight yet. Once again, I thought I was dreaming."

❦ Chapter 23 ❧

A New Job for Ryan

Six months after Sarah's wedding, Ryan was busy managing the 29th Street renovation project. The storeowners and tenants along a five-block section really liked his ideas, and unanimously* decided to hire him. Some business owners wanted only minor adjustments, such as the addition of trees, bushes, or flower boxes. Others chose more elaborate* touches, like fountains, awnings*, decks, patios, and walkways. Needless to say, Ryan's creativity and attention to detail had a very positive result. First and foremost, the dramatic changes made the whole area look much more appealing.

The *Times Journal* did a story about the street's redevelopment. The article drew a lot of attention, and brought new customers to the area. It also attracted new businesses to the community. Within three months, an old, abandoned building around the corner from *Julio's Flower Shop* was inhabited by three new establishments: a coffee house, a clothing boutique, and a bookstore. The neighborhood on and around 29th Street was actually becoming very fashionable.

Luisa was correct about the job being a huge professional break for Ryan. Soon, he was receiving contracts from other blocks in the neighborhood—and all over the city. "I no longer have time to fulfill all of my gardener duties in Oak Hills," he joked. "*Soto Landscape Architecture* may actually need another employee or two."

"Don't look at me, sweetheart," said Luisa. "I'm much too busy at the shop to worry about your roses—or anything else at the estate." Luisa was indeed very busy. Since Sarah's wedding, *Julio's Flower Shop* had handled several high-end social events in addition to their growing walk-in business. Luisa had also had to add another full-time employee to her staff.

Nevertheless, Ryan and Luisa were quite determined to make time for each other. They regularly met in Oak Hills, on 29th Street, or somewhere in between. They talked on the phone daily. They got better acquainted* with the people in their respective families. Although Mrs. Brooks—now *Amanda*—did remain something of a mystery, Luisa grew to respect and, yes, even like her. From time to time, Amanda came down from Oak Hills to inspect the project on 29th Street. Then they all had lunch together in the studio. It was on one of those days that she revealed to Luisa more about her personal history.

Amanda Brooks was very young when she married Ryan's father, Alberto Soto. They lived close to Ryan's other relatives on 31st Street. Amanda stayed home and took care of Ryan, while her husband taught math at a high school. He strongly encouraged his students to get a higher education—especially the many lower-income Hispanic kids in his classes. "Don't find yourselves mowing someone else's lawn someday," he used to say. "Get an education. Give yourself the opportunity of a brighter future."

Mrs. Brooks' voice cracked with emotion when she talked about his accident. "It was dark," she said. "He was on a bicycle on his way home from school. He was hit by a car and died just a few blocks from here—over on 32nd Street. For many years, I couldn't bear to come near this area."

Ryan was only four years old when the accident happened. Her parents insisted that she and Ryan move back in with them. Two years later, she married William Brooks, a junior partner in a big technology company. In a few years, her second husband had made millions. Fortunately, it was a very good marriage, and he was a wonderful stepfather to Ryan. They had a beautiful daughter and spent many happy years together—until he got sick. "I was devastated," said Mrs. Brooks. "And I became bitter and unhappy. Thank goodness I had the support of my two wonderful children. I don't know what I would have done without them."

It wasn't the first time that Luisa had reflected back on the conversation she had with her mother. Beatriz, of course, was right: *No one knows what she's been through in life—or what she's going through now. But there is something you should know: first impressions can be completely wrong.* Mrs. Brooks then added, "You know, after that choking incident, I developed a new perspective* about life. I realized that it wasn't worth wasting another moment being angry and miserable."

"Right, Mom," said Ryan, winking. "You realized that there were more important things in life than your marble floors."

"And yet," said Mrs. Brooks. "I do *like* my marble floors. Please, *please*, try to remember to leave your work boots outside."

❧ Chapter 24 ❧

A Floral Arrangement

Three and a half years later, Ryan was in the rose garden in Oak Hills. It was a beautiful afternoon in June. He was wearing his jeans, an old *Soto Landscape Architecture* T-shirt, and his very dirty work boots. Even though Ryan's professional life had made a significant leap, he still loved checking on his precious rose bushes, now tended by a few additional gardeners. This year an extraordinary pink variety had just bloomed. It was his own hybrid creation: the *Luisa*. It was named, of course, for the love of his life— and now his wife—Luisa Sánchez Soto.

Beatriz and Pedro regularly came up to the estate to visit their daughter and her husband. They were delighted to see Luisa and Ryan settled in the caretaker's cottage. Compared to the Brooks Mansion, perhaps it could be described as a cottage. In reality, however, it was a lovely four-bedroom, three-bathroom home that was almost as elegant as the main house. Because Ryan had designed it, he left out the marble floors. They were far too high-maintenance for him. Instead, he chose Mexican Saltillo tiles that were covered here and there with beautiful woolen rugs.

Mrs. Brooks, too, was delighted that her son and daughter-in-law continued to live on the estate. Of course, Ryan and Luisa had to go back and forth to the city. And sometimes they were too tired to return, opting* instead to stay the night in Luisa's old apartment above *Julio's Flower Shop*. The convenience of the arrangement suited them both very well.

After Ryan and Luisa were married, the estate in Oak Hills also helped support them. Several new flower gardens were planted on the estate, and a large greenhouse was built to grow other exotic plants. These flowers and plants were regularly used both in Ryan's business and in Luisa's. In June, for example, *Julio's Flower Shop* bought very few roses from their wholesaler. Instead, they were cut from their own rose garden, and hardly missed. Mrs. Brooks, in fact, enjoyed the thought of her flowers being shared all over the city. "Just tell your customers that they're from the Brooks Nursery," she said. "And then charge them a bit extra."

Tia Teresa and her employees were thriving. They had become the most popular Mexican food caterer in the city. Her staff grew to include just about every relative and friend of the family. She considered opening her own Mexican restaurant somewhere around 29th Street. "I'd love to move in near *Julio's*," she said. "But this neighborhood has become a bit too trendy*. I may just buy a place closer to 7th Avenue."

After Ryan had cut twelve of the *Luisa* roses from their bush, he returned to the caretaker's cottage. He stomped the dirt from his work shoes and opened the door, but then he decided not to walk into the house before taking them off. Both his mother and his wife agreed that the boots were never allowed inside. Ryan argued that the additional scratches in the Saltillo tile "added character" to the floor. "This is our home, Ryan," said Luisa, firmly. "Let's try to keep it clean."

Ryan walked into the kitchen and set the roses down on the table. With the tool in his pocket, he painstakingly* removed all the thorns. He opened a cabinet, selected a tall vase, and filled it up with water. Finally, one by one, he put the roses into the vase. Then he opened a drawer, cut a piece of silk ribbon, wound it around the center of the vase, and tied it into a bow. "Beautiful," he thought, as he turned the arrangement around on the kitchen counter,

Ryan found Luisa sitting in a rocking chair with their one-week-old daughter, Rosa.

inspecting it from every angle. "Perfect for the mother of a new baby girl."

Ryan washed his hands and quietly walked into their bedroom. He found Luisa sitting in a rocking chair with their one-week-old daughter, Rosa.

The sight of his wife and baby gave him a lump in his throat. He smiled and put the roses on the nightstand next to the bed.

"What do you think? Does it look professional?" he asked, gently scooping the baby out of her mother's arms and into his own.

"You are an amazing florist, husband, and father," Luisa said, standing up and putting her arms around him. Luisa looked at both her husband and daughter adoringly.

"And who do you think Rosa looks like today?" Ryan asked, smiling at the wide-awake baby.

"Neither one of us, really," said Luisa with a huge grin. "Take a good look at her, Ryan. It's obvious, isn't it?"

"I suppose so," said Ryan, laughing. "She looks exactly like my mother."

❧ E X E R C I S E S ❧

Ⓐ Comprehension

Chapters 1 – 6 Write short answers to the following questions.

  1 Why did Luisa go back to *Julio's Flower Shop* after university?

  2 Why was Luisa nervous about going to Oak Hills?

  3 What were Luisa's first impressions of Ryan and Mrs. Brooks?

  4 Why was their children's education so important to Pedro and Beatriz Sánchez?

  5 Why was Beatriz worried about her daughter falling in love with a gardener?

  6 What do the expressions *'Rome wasn't built in a day'* and *'her bark is worse than her bite'* mean? Who or what was Ryan referring to when he said them?

Chapters 7 – 12 Who said the following sentences? Choose the correct option.

  7 "Never mind. Come in. Sarah has been waiting for you."
    a. Mrs. Brooks   **b**. Ryan   **c.** Beatriz

  8 "Well, people don't actually die of embarrassment, like they sometimes do from choking."
    a. Mrs. Brooks   **b**. Sarah   **c.** Luisa

  9 "There is nothing you can say to those idiots, Luisa. Just ignore them."
    a. Mrs. Brooks   **b**. Ryan   **c.** Pedro

 10 "We are now *legally* obliged to carry out the service we promised to deliver."
    a. Katya   **b**. Beatriz   **c.** Pedro

 11 "On the telephone, I didn't hear the monster you've described."
    a. Beatriz   **b**. Luisa   **c.** Emma

 12 "She might take it the wrong way."
    a. Mrs. Brooks   **b**. Pedro   **c.** Luisa

Chapters 13 – 18 Are the following sentences true or false? Choose the correct option.

13 Mrs. Brooks does not like Beatriz Sánchez's food.   **T / F**

14 Mrs. Brooks refuses to let Beatriz give Ryan any food. **T / F**

15 Ryan is annoyed by Luisa's questions about Mrs. Brooks. **T / F**

16 Luisa is not excited about her date with Ryan.   **T / F**

17 Pedro is very encouraging about Ryan's business.   **T / F**

18 Ryan's mother appears in these chapters.   **T / F**

Chapters 19 – 24 Write answers to the following questions.

19 Why was Luisa so surprised that Sarah was marrying a Mexican man?

20 Luisa thought that Ryan wasn't allowed in the house because he was Latino. What was the real reason?

21 What changed Luisa's impression of Mrs. Brooks?

22 Why did Ryan lie to Luisa about his background?

23 What difficult events in Mrs. Brooks' life made her so bitter and unpleasant?

24 How did Ryan's business benefit *Julio's Flower Shop* at the end of the story?

B Working with Language

1 Complete the following sentences from *A Floral Arrangement* with words from the box.

deserving	over-the-top	freshly-ironed	to overhear
proud	matching	longer	tasteful	bitterness

1 Luisa no _____ felt angry. How was it possible to feel _____ toward the people who had helped her pay her way through college?

2 I'm _____ to say we've given academic scholarships to hundreds of _____ kids.

3 She definitely didn't want anyone _____ this telephone conversation.

4 The floral arrangements were lavish but very _____.

5 She put on her black skirt, _____ jacket, and a _____ white blouse.

6 I don't want this wedding to be too _____ I'd be fine with something simple.

2 Match the sentence halves.

1 I wish

2 If we refuse to honor the contract

3 In spite of her resentment towards Mrs. Brooks,

4 I am allowed in the house as long as

5 Luisa didn't retaliate with nasty remarks,

6 If it weren't for her ugly behavior,

a Luisa jumped out of her chair and ran to her side.

b I don't sit down on the nicer furniture.

c she will call her attorneys and take us to court.

d Mrs. Brooks might have been a very pretty older woman.

e she would come up again for a visit.

f she swallowed her pride and said nothing.

C Activities

1 Imagine you are having a conversation with somebody and you think they have made a racist comment. How does it make you feel? Do you do or say anything?

2 Luisa forgives Ryan even though he has lied to her throughout their relationship. Write an email from Luisa to a friend, explaining what happened and why you forgave Ryan.

3 "First impressions can be completely wrong." Think of a situation in your experience when this has been true, and a situation when first impressions were correct.

GLOSSARY

abrasive *(adj)* acting in a rude and unkind manner

accomplish *(vb)* to succeed in completing something

acquainted *(adj)* familiar with something or someone

ancestry *(n)* the family of people that you come from

awning *(n)* a sheet of strong cloth that keeps the sun or rain off doors or windows

barrette *(n)* a hair-slide

blue-collar job *(n)* a manual job, like a gardener, factory worker, mechanic, etc.

bouquet *(n)* a bunch of flowers

boutonniere *(n)* a small flower worn on a man's jacket

browbeat *(vb)* to frighten or threaten someone until they do something

cascading *(adj)* flowing downwards in large amounts

chauffeur *(n)* someone who is paid to drive a car

composure *(n)* the state of being calm and in control of yourself

condescending *(adj)* behaving as if you are more important or intelligent than others

contempt *(n)* the feeling that something or someone has no value and deserves no respect

corsage *(n)* a small bunch of flowers that a woman wears on her dress, e.g. for a wedding

courteous *(adj)* polite, respectful

coward *(n)* a person who is not brave

crush *(n)* a feeling of attraction, which doesn't last very long

curtly *(avb)* in a manner that is short, and usually rude

deceased *(adj)* if someone is deceased it means they have died

degrading *(adj)* treating somebody as if they have no value

demoralizing *(adj)* in a way that makes somebody lose confidence or hope

disdainfully *(adv)* in a way that shows a person has no respect for another

dishonorable *(adj)* immoral; not deserving respect

donor *(n)* a person or organization that gives money to a charity or foundation

elaborate *(adj)* very complicated and detailed

elitist *(n)* a person who thinks they are better than people of a lower social class

enigma *(n)* something or someone mysterious and difficult to understand

enterprising *(adj)* having the ability to think of new ways to do things

entrepreneur *(n)* a person who makes money by starting or running businesses

foundation *(n)* an organization that provides money for a particular purpose, such as charity

foyer *(n)* In a theatre or hotel, for example, the foyer is a large space where people can wait. In a private house, the foyer is the entrance hall.

generation *(n)* a stage in the history of a family, e.g. grandparents, parents or children

grueling *(adj)* very difficult and exhausting, requiring a great deal of effort

Heimlich Maneuver *(n)* a procedure for removing the blockage that's causing someone to choke

high-maintenance *(adj)* needing a lot of attention

horticulture *(n)* the study or practice of growing plants

hostile *(adj)* unfriendly; showing dislike

ignite *(vb)* to set off, inflame

incompetent *(adj)* not having the necessary skills to complete a task successfully

indifferently *(adv)* without having strong feelings

inexplicably *(adv)* in a way that can't be understood or explained

infuriated *(adj)* extremely angry

intercom *(n)* an electrical device that allows one- or two-way communication within a house, office etc.

lavish *(adj)* luxurious

legacy *(n)* something left to one's child or successor

mansion *(n)* an enormous, luxurious house

mischievously *(adv)* causing trouble in a playful way

mogul *(n)* an important or powerful person

opt *(vb)* to choose

painstakingly *(avb)* with great care

peon *(n)* a person who does boring, low-paid work

perspective *(n)* a particular way of thinking about something

portable *(adj)* easy to move around

portfolio *(n)* a flat case for carrying loose papers

predicament *(n)* a difficult or unpleasant situation

rampage *(n)* a period of violent and uncontrollable behavior

recruit *(vb)* to persuade someone to do something for you, usually to work for you

resentment *(n)* negative feelings e.g. about being treated unfairly

resolve *(n)* when you have made a firm decision about something

retaliate *(vb)* to make an attack in response to a similar attack

scholarship *(n)* a payment made by an organization to support a student's education

serenade *(vb)* to play music, often to someone one loves or admires

shears *(n)* large scissors used for gardening

spectacular *(adj)* extremely impressive

sternly *(adv)* strictly; with severity

submissive *(adj)* obedient, too willing to accept the authority of others

tedious *(adj)* extremely boring

testimonial *(n)* a statement that vouches for the value of something

thunderstruck *(adj)* extremely shocked, usually in a negative way

toss *(vb)* to throw

trendy *(adj)* very fashionable

unanimously *(adv)* if every person involved in a decision agrees, it is unanimous

wince *(vb)* to make an involuntary expression as a result of pain or embarrassment

A N S W E R   K E Y

🄰 Comprehension

Chapters 1 – 6

1 Luisa went back because she was devoted to the family legacy.

2 Luisa was nervous because she was not used to having such rich clients with such enormous houses.

3 Luisa liked Ryan straight away, but thought that Mrs. Brooks was rude and elitist.

4 It was important to them because it would give their children the best chance at a successful life, which Beatriz and Pedro had not had.

5 Beatriz was worried because she thought that Luisa would eventually resent Ryan for not making much money.

6 *'Rome wasn't built in a day'* means that something great takes a long time to achieve – it doesn't happen quickly. Ryan was referring to his business. *'Her bark is worse than her bite'* means that someone isn't as aggressive as they sound or seem. Ryan was referring to Mrs. Brooks.

Chapters 7 – 12

7 a   **8** b   **9** c   **10** b   **11** a   **12** c

Chapters 13 – 18

13 F   **14** T   **15** F   **16** F   **17** T   **18** T

Chapters 19 – 24

19 She was surprised because she had assumed up until now that Mrs. Brooks hated Mexicans.

20 The real reason was that Mrs. Brooks didn't want Ryan's boots scratching her marble floor.

21 Luisa's opinion changed because of Mrs. Brooks' attachment to the Alberto Soto Foundation.

22 Ryan lied so that he could see what Luisa thought of his personality rather than his money.

23 The deaths of both of her husbands made Mrs. Brooks bitter and unpleasant.

24 Ryan's business benefited the flower shop because they could use Ryan's beautiful roses instead of buying roses from the wholesaler.

B Working with Language

1

  1 longer, bitterness
  2 proud, deserving
  3 to overhear
  4 tasteful
  5 matching, freshly-ironed
  6 over-the-top

2

  1 e **2** c **3** a **4** b **5** f **6** d

C Activities

Students' own answers